Table of C(

Chapter 1: Introduction

Overview of the concept of hidden gems in France

One such hidden gem is Giverny, a picturesque village located in the Normandy region. Giverny gained fame due to its association with the renowned impressionist painter Claude Monet, who lived and worked there for many years. The main attraction in Giverny is Monet's house and gardens, which served as inspiration for some of his most iconic works, including the famous water lilies series. Visitors can walk through the enchanting garden, admire the vibrant colors and blooming flowers, and even visit Monet's charming pink-painted house. Giverny offers a serene and tranquil atmosphere, transporting visitors back to the time when Monet himself roamed these very grounds.

Another hidden gem in France is the charming town of Rocamadour, nestled high up on a cliff in the Midi-Pyrénées region. Often referred to as a medieval pilgrimage site, Rocamadour boasts a rich history dating back to the 12th century. The town is home to several religious sites, including the Notre-Dame Chapel and the Saint-Sauveur Basilica, which attract pilgrims and tourists alike. The allure of Rocamadour lies not only in its historical significance but also in its breathtaking views. As visitors climb the steep cobblestone streets and stairways, they are rewarded with stunning vistas of the surrounding countryside. The town's unique location and architectural beauty make it a hidden gem worth exploring.

Moving to the northern part of France, the charming city of Colmar emerges as another hidden gem. Situated in the picturesque region of Alsace, Colmar boasts a well-preserved medieval old town with colorful half-timbered houses and charming canals. Known as the "Little Venice of Alsace," visitors can take a boat tour along the canals, admiring the city's architectural splendor and soaking in the romantic atmosphere. Colmar is also famous for its vibrant Christmas markets, which attract visitors from all over the world. The combination of the city's enchanting architecture, rich history, and festive spirit makes Colmar an unforgettable hidden gem.

Moreover, France is not only renowned for its cities and towns but also for its natural landscapes, and the Verdon Gorge is a prime example of this. Often referred to as the "Grand Canyon of Europe," the Verdon Gorge is a breathtaking river canyon located in southeastern France. With its towering limestone cliffs, crystal-clear turquoise waters, and dramatic scenery, the Verdon Gorge offers a paradise for adventure enthusiasts. Visitors can engage in activities such as kayaking, hiking, rock climbing, and even paragliding, taking in the awe-inspiring beauty of the surroundings. The Verdon Gorge is a hidden gem that showcases the diverse and stunning natural landscapes France has to offer.

As we delve into the concept of hidden gems in France, it becomes evident that this country is not solely defined by its iconic landmarks. Behind the widely known attractions lie numerous hidden treasures waiting to be discovered. Whether it's exploring Monet's garden in Giverny, ascending the cliffs of Rocamadour, strolling along the canals of Colmar, or venturing into the Verdon Gorge, each hidden gem unravels a unique story. These lesser-known destinations provide an opportunity to delve deeper into the rich tapestry of French history, culture, and natural beauty. So, the next time you find yourself in France, take a chance, step off the beaten path, and uncover the hidden gems that await you.

Importance of exploring lesser-known destinations

One among primary reasons why it is important to explore lesser-known destinations lies in the sense of discovery and adventure they offer. Travelers are increasingly seeking authentic, off-the-beaten-path experiences that immerse them in the local culture. These destinations often have a more genuine and untouched atmosphere where visitors can encounter local traditions, customs, and cuisines that remain unspoiled by mass tourism. As we venture into these lesser-known corners of the world, our understanding of the diversity and intricacies of human existence deepens, fostering a sense of empathy and appreciation for different ways of life.

Furthermore, exploring lesser-known destinations is crucial for sustainable tourism. Popular tourist hotspots often suffer from overtourism, resulting in overcrowding, environmental degradation, and cultural commodification. By diverting our attention to lesser-known destinations, we alleviate the strain placed on fragile ecosystems and vulnerable communities. This shift not only ensures the preservation of natural and cultural heritage but also promotes responsible tourism practices. As travelers, we have a responsibility to leave a positive impact on the places we visit, and by exploring lesser-known destinations, we can contribute to the sustainability and resilience of those communities.

Another significant aspect worth considering is the economic impact of exploring lesser-known destinations. For many countries and regions, tourism plays a vital role in their economies. However, the concentration of tourists in a few well-known destinations can lead to economic disparities, with many smaller communities and rural areas being left behind. By exploring lesser-known destinations, we can help distribute the economic benefits of tourism more evenly, supporting local businesses, artisans, and entrepreneurs. This, in turn, leads to the development of sustainable livelihoods, job creation, and a stronger sense of community.

Moreover, exploring lesser-known destinations unveils hidden treasures and untold stories that may otherwise remain overlooked. The world is a vast tapestry of diverse landscapes, historical sites, and cultural heritage waiting to be discovered. From ancient temples nestled in remote corners of Southeast Asia to pristine mountain ranges in South America, these lesser-known destinations have the capacity to surprise and captivate us. By venturing beyond the familiar, we uncover lesser-known historical events, traditions, and art forms that paint a richer and more nuanced picture of our shared human history. These discoveries challenge our assumptions and expand our worldview, promoting intercultural understanding and fostering dialogue. By embracing the spirit of adventure and curiosity, we can uncover unique experiences that showcase the true essence of a place. In doing so, we contribute to sustainable tourism practices by alleviating the strain on popular destinations. Exploring lesser-known destinations also has a positive economic impact, supporting local communities and distributing the benefits of tourism more equitably. Most importantly, it allows us to discover hidden treasures and untold stories, ultimately enriching our lives and broadening our perspectives. So, let us open our minds and wander off the beaten path, for it is in the exploration of lesser-known destinations that we find the true essence of travel.

Chapter 2: A Taste of the Countryside

Charming villages and towns off the beaten path

Imagine wandering down cobblestone streets lined with centuries-old houses, breathing in the scent of freshly baked bread wafting from local bakeries, and hearing the cheerful chatter of locals going about their daily routines. This is the allure of exploring charming villages and towns off the beaten path. Away from the tourist hotspots, these hidden treasures often exude an undeniably authentic atmosphere that is hard to replicate in more cosmopolitan cities.

One such enchanting destination is the picturesque village of Hallstatt in Austria. Nestled in the stunning Salzkammergut region, Hallstatt is a mesmerizing blend of pristine natural landscapes and a well-preserved UNESCO World Heritage-listed town. This serene village is a postcard-perfect scene, with its traditional Alpine houses reflecting on the calm waters of Lake Hallstatt. It offers visitors the opportunity to immerse themselves in the tranquility of the Austrian countryside while exploring charming streets dotted with artisan shops, quaint cafes, and intriguing museums.

Venturing further into Europe, the fairytale village of Giethoorn in the Netherlands beckons with its idyllic canals and enchanting thatched-roof cottages. Known as the "Venice of the Netherlands," this car-free village transports visitors into a bygone era, where the only means of transportation is by boat or on foot. As you paddle along the narrow canals, you'll discover hidden corners and small bridges that add to the village's undeniable charm. Giethoorn is an ideal destination for those seeking a peaceful respite and a chance to appreciate the simplicity and beauty of rural life.

Beyond Europe, the charming town of Luang Prabang in Laos offers a unique blend of colonial architecture, vibrant temples, and serene surroundings. Situated amidst mountains and at the confluence of the Mekong and Nam Khan rivers, Luang Prabang boasts a tranquil ambiance that is truly captivating. Its UNESCO World Heritage designation is a testament to the town's rich cultural heritage, with ornate temples and former royal palaces standing as testament to the grandeur of the past. Luang Prabang also offers visitors the opportunity to witness and participate in the daily ritual of tak bat, where monks walk the streets at dawn to receive alms, a cultural experience that is both humbling and awe-inspiring.

Further afield, the coastal village of Kinsale in Ireland offers an irresistible blend of history, beauty, and culinary delights. Nestled in County Cork, Kinsale showcases its rich maritime heritage through narrow, winding streets lined with colorful buildings that house charming shops and gourmet restaurants. As you stroll along the harbor, you'll be greeted by the aroma of freshly caught seafood being prepared in the town's numerous award-winning restaurants. Kinsale also offers history enthusiasts the opportunity to explore Charles Fort, a 17th-century star-shaped fort that played a pivotal role in Irish history. Whether it's meandering down cobblestone streets in Hallstatt, gliding through the canals of Giethoorn, witnessing the cultural richness of Luang Prabang, or immersing oneself in the maritime beauty of Kinsale, these offbeat destinations offer a chance to slow down and connect with the true spirit of a place. Through this book, we invite you to embark on a journey to discover these hidden gems and uncover the true treasures that lie off the beaten path.

Unique countryside experiences in France

From charming villages nestled amidst rolling hills to picturesque vineyards and tranquil nature reserves, the French countryside has something for everyone. In this article, we will explore some of the most extraordinary and off-the-beaten-path experiences that France has to offer, allowing visitors to fully immerse themselves in the beauty and authenticity of rural France.

Village Retreats:
A part of most enchanting aspects of the French countryside is its quaint villages that seem to have stood still in time. These idyllic hamlets offer a truly unique experience, providing visitors with an opportunity to disconnect from the hustle and bustle of everyday life. From the stone-clad houses of Alsace to the lavender-filled fields of Provence, each village offers its own distinct charm and character. Strolling through narrow, cobblestone streets, discovering charming cafes and local artisan shops, and engaging with friendly locals are just some of the highlights awaiting visitors to these picturesque villages.

Wine and Gastronomy:
A trip to the French countryside wouldn't be complete without indulging in the country's world-renowned wine and gastronomy. France boasts numerous wine regions, including Bordeaux, Burgundy, Champagne, and the Loire Valley, each offering unique tasting experiences. Visitors can explore vineyards, learn about winemaking traditions, and sample a variety of exquisite wines. Additionally, the French countryside is home to an abundance of farm-to-table restaurants and traditional markets, where one can savor the freshest locally-sourced ingredients and engage with passionate producers. These culinary experiences are a true reflection of the French way of life, rooted in a deep appreciation for food and wine.

Outdoor Adventures:
For those seeking outdoor thrills, the French countryside offers a plethora of activities set amidst stunning natural landscapes. From hiking along the rugged coastline of Brittany to horseback riding through the lavender fields of Provence, the options are endless. Nature reserves, such as the Camargue and the Cevennes, provide opportunities for wildlife spotting, birdwatching, and exploring diverse ecosystems. Canoeing down the picturesque rivers of the Dordogne or the Ardèche is another exciting way to experience the countryside. Adventure enthusiasts can also tackle the challenging terrain of the French Alps, with world-class skiing and mountaineering opportunities.

Historical and Cultural Immersion:
France's countryside is steeped in history and culture, with countless châteaux, medieval towns, and ancient ruins waiting to be discovered. Perched on hilltops overlooking the countryside, these architectural wonders offer visitors a glimpse into the past

and a chance to marvel at their grandeur. Exploring fortified cities like Carcassonne or wandering through the medieval streets of Sarlat will transport travelers back in time. Additionally, museums dedicated to local traditions, arts, and crafts offer a deeper understanding of the rich cultural heritage of the region. From tapestry workshops in Normandy to porcelain factories in Limoges, these immersive experiences allow visitors to appreciate the intricate craftsmanship that has shaped the French countryside.

France's unique countryside experiences provide an exceptional opportunity to connect with nature, immerse oneself in the local culture, and rejuvenate the soul. Whether savoring the delights of a charming village, indulging in wine and gastronomy, exploring nature's wonders, or delving into the historical and cultural treasures, the French countryside leaves an indelible mark on visitors. With its extraordinary blend of authenticity, beauty, and diversity, the French countryside invites travelers to embark on unforgettable journeys that will forever be etched in their memories. Begin your own exploration of this remarkable land and create memories that will last a lifetime.

Chapter 3: Coastal Treasures

Lesser-known coastal destinations in France

First on our list is the picturesque town of Honfleur, located in the Normandy region of northern France. Nestled along the Seine estuary, Honfleur enchants visitors with its charming harbor, colorful buildings, and cobblestone streets. Its historic importance as a significant trading port is evident in its well-preserved architecture, reminiscent of the medieval era. Walking along the Vieux Bassin, Honfleur's iconic harbor, you'll be captivated by the vibrant reflections of the tall, narrow buildings on the water. Explore the quaint shops, art galleries, and sample the local seafood delicacies in the charming cafes that line the harbor.

Moving along the Atlantic coast, we arrive at the serene île de Ré. Located off the western coast of France, this idyllic island offers a peaceful and relaxing retreat. Known for its sandy beaches, picturesque villages, and salt marshes, île de Ré is a haven for nature lovers and beach enthusiasts. With over 100 kilometers of cycling paths, renting a bike is the best way to explore the island and soak in its natural beauty. Don't miss out on visiting the medieval town of Saint-Martin-de-Ré, with its impressive fortifications and charming marina. Experience the peacefulness of île de Ré by indulging in locally produced oysters, the island's delicacy.

Further down the Atlantic coast, we discover the fascinating Belle-île-en-Mer. This charming island, located in the region of Brittany, is the largest of the Breton islands. Famous for its rugged coastline, breathtaking cliffs, and pristine beaches, Belle-île-en-Mer exudes a wild and untamed beauty. Take a stroll along the coastal path known as the "Sentier des Douaniers," which offers splendid views of the Atlantic Ocean and hidden coves. Admire the striking Citadelle Vauban, a fortress built by Vauban, the famous military architect. Complete your visit by exploring the charming village of Le Palais, the island's main town.

Heading south to the Mediterranean coastline, we encounter the enchanting town of Collioure. Situated in the Occitanie region, near the Spanish border, Collioure embodies the perfect blend of French and Catalan cultures. Its rich history as a fishing village and an artistic hub attracts visitors from around the world. Stroll through the charming streets adorned with vibrant colors, visit the imposing Château Royal de Collioure, and relax at one of the numerous seaside cafes. Collioure's unique charm has inspired many artists, including Henri Matisse and Pablo Picasso, who spent time in the town and created masterpieces inspired by its beauty.

Continuing our journey along the Mediterranean coast, we arrive at the captivating town of Cassis. Nestled between Marseille and Toulon, Cassis is blessed with stunning landscapes that will leave you in awe. The sparkling turquoise waters of the Mediterranean contrast beautifully with the towering white limestone cliffs known as the "Calanques." These dramatic natural formations are best explored by taking a boat tour, providing a unique perspective of Cassis's breathtaking coastline. Don't miss the opportunity to savor the local cuisine, especially the renowned white wine and fresh seafood, which Cassis is famous for. Whether it's the picturesque harbor of Honfleur, the peacefulness of île de Ré, the wild beauty of Belle-île-en-Mer, the blend of cultures in Collioure, or the stunning landscapes of Cassis, these hidden gems are waiting to be discovered. Venture beyond the popular tourist destinations and immerse yourself in the charm, history, and natural beauty of these lesser-known coastal destinations in France. Your journey will be rewarded with unforgettable memories and an appreciation for the hidden treasures that this captivating country has to offer.

Hidden beaches and scenic coastal views

A single most enchanting aspects of hidden beaches is their elusive nature. Tucked away from mainstream tourist destinations, these beaches offer a sense of exclusivity and tranquility that is often hard to find elsewhere. Picture yourself on a remote island, walking along an untouched strip of sand, with the only sounds being the gentle lapping of waves and the distant call of seagulls. This is the kind of experience that hidden beaches offer— an escape from the hustle and bustle of everyday life and an opportunity to reconnect with nature in its purest form.

But what makes these hidden beaches truly special is their ability to surprise and delight us with their unique features and breathtaking beauty. While popular beaches may boast grandeur and amenities, hidden beaches reveal a raw and unspoiled beauty that feels like a privilege to witness. From the dramatic cliffs of Portugal's Algarve coast to the pristine turquoise waters of the Seychelles, each hidden beach has its own story to tell, its own landscape to share. These beaches often showcase extraordinary rock formations, secret caves, or hidden waterfalls, creating a sense of discovery and awe that is unparalleled.

Beyond their picturesque beauty, hidden beaches also offer a variety of activities that cater to different interests. Whether you are an adventure seeker looking for adrenaline-pumping water sports, a nature lover yearning to explore marine life through snorkeling or scuba diving, or simply seeking a peaceful spot for a romantic getaway, these hidden beaches have it all. Imagine kayaking through crystal-clear waters, exploring hidden coves accessible only by sea, or simply basking in the sun on soft sands as you soak in the breathtaking coastal views. The possibilities are endless, and each hidden beach promises a unique experience tailored to your desires.

While visiting hidden beaches can be an incredible experience, it's essential to approach these places with respect and mindfulness. Many of these locations are still pristine because of their limited exposure to tourism and human impact. As travelers, it is our responsibility to preserve the integrity of these hidden gems and minimize our ecological footprint. Embracing sustainable tourism practices, such as avoiding littering, respecting local flora and fauna, and supporting local communities, can help ensure the longevity of these extraordinary destinations for generations to come.

In this book, we will take you on a virtual tour to some of the world's most captivating hidden beaches and scenic coastal views. From remote stretches of sand along the rugged Pacific Coast of California to hidden coves nestled in the lush rainforests of Costa Rica, we will explore a diverse range of destinations that hold secrets waiting to be uncovered. Through inspiring narratives, captivating photographs, and practical tips, we hope to ignite your wanderlust, empower you with the knowledge to plan your own adventure, and ultimately help you discover the hidden beaches and scenic coastal views that will leave an indelible mark on your travel memories. So, gear up for an unforgettable journey as we embark on this exploration of hidden paradises you never knew existed.

Chapter 4: Historic Marvels

Discovering lesser-known historical sites in France

While iconic destinations like the Eiffel Tower, Louvre Museum, and Palace of Versailles undoubtedly captivate visitors, there is a treasure trove of lesser-known historical sites waiting to be discovered. These hidden gems not only provide a deeper insight into France's past but also offer a unique and intimate experience away from the crowds. In this exploration, we will delve into the enchanting world of lesser-known historical sites in France, unveiling their untold stories and inviting you to embark on a journey of discovery.

1. The Abbey of Jumièges:

Our expedition begins in the heart of Normandy, where the Abbey of Jumièges stands as an impressive testament to the region's medieval heritage. Nestled amidst picturesque landscapes, the abbey traces its origins back to the 7th century. Though partially in ruins today, the site exudes a remarkable aura of tranquility, allowing visitors to admire the grandeur of its Romanesque architecture. Take a leisurely stroll through the ancient corridors, meander along the beautifully landscaped gardens, and soak in the profound spirituality of this hidden gem.

2. The Fortified City of Carcassonne:

Embarking on an adventure to southern France, we find ourselves in the enchanting city of Carcassonne. Enclosed within its towering ramparts, the fortified city is reminiscent of a medieval fairytale. This UNESCO World Heritage site showcases a perfectly preserved medieval citadel, complete with cobbled streets, fortified walls, and imposing watchtowers. Step through the gates of history as you wander the narrow alleys, contemplate the intricate defensive architecture, and bask in the authenticity of a bygone era.

3. The Château de Vincennes:

Heading towards the outskirts of Paris, we encounter the splendid Château de Vincennes. Often overlooked by visitors, this medieval fortress is a true hidden gem. Its fascinating history stretches back to the 14th century, serving as a royal residence, hunting lodge, and a state prison. Explore its grand halls, gaze upon the soaring keep, and imagine the vibrant court life that animated its walls. The château's proximity to Paris makes it an ideal day trip for those seeking to immerse themselves in France's legendary past.

4. The Lascaux Caves:

Venturing into prehistoric times, we journey to southwestern France to unearth a marvel of Paleolithic art — the Lascaux Caves. Discovered in 1940, these caves house some of the most extraordinary examples of prehistoric cave paintings ever found. While the original caves are now closed to the public to preserve their delicate environment, an impeccable replica allows visitors to experience the awe-inspiring artistry firsthand. Marvel at the intricate depictions of beasts and human figures, and uncover the mysteries left behind by our ancestors.

5. The Pont du Gard:

Transporting us to the Roman era, we arrive at the stunning Pont du Gard, an ancient aqueduct nestled in the sun-kissed region of Provence. This awe-inspiring structure spans the Gardon River and stands as an emblem of Roman engineering prowess. Built in the 1st century AD, the bridge served as a vital artery, providing water to the nearby town of Nîmes. Today, visitors can not only marvel at the grandeur of the aqueduct but also explore the surrounding verdant landscapes and take a refreshing dip in the river.

France is undoubtedly a treasure trove for history enthusiasts, offering a wealth of lesser-known historical sites waiting to be explored. From medieval abbeys to fortified cities, from ancient cave art to Roman engineering marvels, each of these hidden gems provides a unique opportunity to delve deeper into France's rich cultural tapestry. By venturing beyond the well-trodden paths and discovering these lesser-known sites, you'll uncover fascinating stories, engage with local history, and create unforgettable memories. So, pack your curiosity and embark on an enchanting journey to unravel the lesser-known historical sites of France.

Cultural significance of hidden historic gems

Exploring hidden historic gems allows us to uncover stories that have been overshadowed or neglected, shedding light on lesser-known ones of history. These hidden gems may consist of forgotten ruins, underground tunnels, or abandoned villages, each with its distinctive tale waiting to be discovered. By delving into their history, we can gain a deeper understanding of the various societies and civilizations that have left their mark on the world.

A piece of notable advantages of hidden historic gems is their ability to provide insights into marginalized or underrepresented cultures. Often, well-known historic sites focus primarily on prominent civilizations, such as ancient Egypt or Rome. However, hidden gems allow us to explore lesser-known cultures, shedding light on diverse perspectives and narratives that are often overlooked. By uncovering these hidden treasures, we can foster a more inclusive and comprehensive understanding of our world's rich and varied past.

Moreover, hidden historic gems contribute to preserving cultural heritage that may otherwise be lost to time. These hidden sites often lay undiscovered, their historical relevance gradually fading away. By recognizing and highlighting these hidden gems, we can ensure their preservation and promote their significance within the cultural fabric of society. Through conservation efforts, these unrecognized sites can be protected for future generations, maintaining a tangible link to our past.

Hidden historic gems also provide an opportunity for local communities to embrace and promote their cultural identity. Often tucked away in quaint towns and villages, these hidden treasures give communities a chance to showcase their history, attracting tourists and fostering a sense of pride and belonging. Local residents can become ambassadors for their heritage, sharing stories and traditions that may have otherwise gone unnoticed. This engagement with hidden historic gems cultivates a sense of cultural appreciation and a desire to safeguard these treasures for generations to come.

In addition to their cultural significance, hidden historic gems offer a sense of adventure and discovery. Exploring these lesser-known sites can be an exciting and educational experience, allowing visitors to engage with history firsthand. Whether it's stumbling upon an ancient temple in a remote jungle or uncovering hidden chambers beneath a city, these hidden gems offer a sense of awe and wonder that can invigorate our curiosity for the past. Their elusive nature adds an element of mystery, making each exploration all the more captivating.

It is essential to recognize and promote the cultural significance of hidden historic gems to ensure their preservation and the sharing of their stories. By celebrating these hidden treasures, we can promote the diversity and richness of our collective global heritage, fostering a greater understanding and appreciation of the complexities of our shared human history. Let us embark on a journey of discovery, unraveling the tales of forgotten civilizations and embracing the hidden gems that lie waiting to be explored.

Chapter 5: Culinary Delights

Uncovering hidden culinary gems in France

From delicate pastries and artisanal cheeses to exquisite wines and world-class cuisine, the nation's food culture is deeply rooted in tradition and sophistication. While many visitors flock to Paris or Lyon to indulge in the famous dishes and iconic restaurants, there is a whole world of hidden culinary gems throughout the country waiting to be discovered. These hidden treasures offer a unique and authentic experience, often showcasing local specialties and regional culinary traditions. In this book, we will explore the lesser-known culinary destinations in France, uncovering their rich gastronomic heritage and introducing readers to a world of undiscovered flavors and culinary experiences.

Unveiling the Secrets of Provence:
Provence, located in the southeast of France, is a region brimming with culinary delights. Far away from the bustling streets of Paris, this sun-kissed region boasts a wide variety of fresh and seasonal ingredients that form the foundation of Provençal cuisine. In this one, we will explore the charming village markets, where locals and visitors come together to savor the abundance of produce, such as vibrant tomatoes, fragrant herbs, and succulent olives. We will dive into traditional dishes like bouillabaisse, ratatouille, and socca, and discover the hidden

gems tucked away in cobblestone streets, where small family-owned restaurants offer authentic Provençal delicacies. From sipping rosé wine under the shade of olive trees to indulging in delicate lavender-infused desserts, Provence is a treasure trove for food lovers.

The Wonders of the Alsace Region:
Nestled on the eastern border of France, the Alsace region is a melting pot of French and German culinary influences. With its rich history and unique geographical location, this area offers a distinctive gastronomic experience. In this one, we will explore the picturesque towns of Strasbourg, Colmar, and Riquewihr, renowned for their timbered houses and exceptional food traditions. Here, the local cuisine seamlessly blends French elegance with the hearty flavors of German cuisine, resulting in dishes like choucroute garnie and flammekueche. We will also delve into the world of Alsatian wine, exploring the region's vineyards and cellars, where exquisite Rieslings and Gewürztraminers are produced. The Alsace region truly captures the essence of France and Germany, offering a unique culinary experience that should not be missed.

Unearthing the Treasures of the Southwest:
In the southwestern part of France lies a culinary haven that often goes unnoticed by tourists. This untapped gastronomic paradise boasts a rich selection of ingredients, from flavorful duck and foie gras to aromatic truffles and indulgent cheeses. In this one, we will travel to the vibrant city of Toulouse, known as the "pink city" for its distinctive brick architecture. Here, we will explore the bustling food markets and discover the region's famous cassoulet, a hearty slow-cooked dish made with white beans, sausage, and various meats. We will also venture into the

vineyards of Bordeaux, renowned for its world-class wines, and witness the unique culinary fusion that occurs in this region. From the delicacy of confit de canard to the richness of Armagnac, the southwest of France is a goldmine of gastronomic wonders.

Unraveling the Mysteries of Corsican Cuisine:
Off the southeastern coast of France lies the enchanting island of Corsica, a hidden gem with its own distinct culinary identity. In this one, we will uncover the secrets of Corsican cuisine, which is heavily influenced by the island's Mediterranean location and its unique mix of French and Italian heritage. We will delve into the fascinating world of charcuterie, where local artisans produce mouth-watering cured meats like lonzu and prisuttu. We will also explore the mountainous interior of the island, where cheese lovers can indulge in creamy brocciu and tangy casgiu merzu. With its pristine coastline and rugged landscapes, Corsica offers a raw and authentic culinary experience, showcasing the island's natural bounty and the passion of its people.

France is not only a country of iconic landmarks and world-class cuisine but a land of hidden culinary gems waiting to be discovered. In this book, we have journeyed through the lesser-known regions of Provence, Alsace, the Southwest, and Corsica, unearthing their culinary treasures and sharing their unique flavors and traditions. From the sun-drenched fields of Provence to the picturesque villages of Alsace and the rugged landscapes of Corsica, these hidden gems offer a glimpse into the diverse and magnificent culinary tapestry of France. Whether you are a seasoned food enthusiast or an adventurous traveler looking for an authentic experience, exploring these hidden culinary gems will surely leave you with a lasting impression and a newfound appreciation for the rich culinary heritage of France.

Regional specialties and hidden gastronomic treasures

Regional specialties and hidden gastronomic treasures are well worth exploring, as they not only offer delightful culinary experiences but also provide insights into the history, traditions, and local lifestyle of a particular area. In this discussion, we will delve into diverse regional specialties and uncover some of the hidden gems that gastronomes can explore and appreciate.

1. The Rich Tapestry of Regional Specialties:
Every region, be it a country, a state, or even a city, possesses its own distinct cuisine owing to a variety of influences such as climate, history, geography, and cultural traditions. From the aromatic spices used in Indian curries to the fresh seafood delicacies of coastal towns in Italy, regional specialties are embedded in the culinary fabric of these places. Such specialties not only provide a culinary identity but also a sense of pride and belonging for the locals.

Exploring regional specialties can be an exciting journey that takes us off the beaten path. The diversity is astounding, ranging from hearty comfort foods like the traditional cassoulet from southwestern France to the tantalizing flavors of spicy Tex-Mex dishes found in the American Southwest. Each region incorporates its local ingredients, cooking techniques, and flavors into these specialties, creating unique and memorable dining experiences for food enthusiasts.

2. Unearthing Hidden Gastronomic Treasures:
While regional specialties are a good starting point, hidden gastronomic treasures often lie tucked away in less explored corners of the world. These hidden gems offer the intrepid food lover a chance to discover authentic, lesser-known dishes that may have been overshadowed by more famous international cuisines.

Delving into the culinary landscape of a region often reveals surprising delicacies. For instance, the small villages of Provence, France, are home to hidden producers who craft exquisite handmade goat cheeses that are virtually unknown outside the region. Similarly, the remote coastal towns of Japan boast charming seaside establishments that serve remarkably fresh and unique seafood dishes, prepared with generations-old techniques and local ingredients.

Exploring hidden gastronomic treasures doesn't always require extensive travel. Even within our local communities, there may be hidden gems waiting to be discovered. These may be tucked away in unassuming cafes, food stalls, or even food trucks serving exquisite dishes that represent the culinary heritage of a particular region.

3. Culinary Tourism: A Gateway to Regional Delights:
Culinary tourism offers a window into regional specialties and hidden gastronomic treasures, making it a fascinating way to learn about different cultures and traditions through food. An increasing number of travelers are seeking immersive food experiences, going beyond the conventional tourist attractions to engage with local cuisine.

Globally recognized food festivals and markets often showcase regional specialties, allowing visitors to sample a plethora of unique dishes. These events provide an opportunity to interact with local producers, chefs, and food enthusiasts who are passionate about showcasing their regional cuisines. From truffle festivals in Italy to chili cook-offs in the southern United States, these culinary events serve as gateways to discovering hidden gastronomic treasures.

Regional specialties and hidden gastronomic treasures represent the culinary diversity and cultural heritage of our world. Exploring these delights takes us on a journey that educates, engages, and delights our senses. Whether we travel to distant lands or seek out hidden gems in our local communities, we can embark on a culinary adventure that will forever enrich our understanding and appreciation of the world's varied gastronomy. So, let us be curious, open-minded, and willing to indulge in these regional specialties and hidden treasures, for they hold the key to a truly unforgettable gastronomic experience.

Chapter 6: Artistic Wonders

Lesser-known art galleries and museums in France

While the Louvre, Musée d'Orsay, and Centre Pompidou are undoubtedly remarkable, they often overshadow the lesser-known art galleries and museums that house hidden treasures across the country. Join us on an extraordinary journey as we venture off the beaten path, delving into the captivating world of France's lesser-known art venues. From the charming villages to the bustling cities, we will uncover the cultural gems that lie hidden, waiting to be discovered.

Hidden Gems in Paris:
Paris, the city of light, is home to an abundance of exquisite art galleries and museums known internationally. However, tucked away amidst its enchanting streets lie lesser-known establishments that offer unique experiences. One such gem is the Musée de la Chasse et de la Nature—the Museum of Hunting and Nature. Delve into the mesmerizing collections celebrating the relationship between humans and animals, presented in a truly artistic manner. Another not-to-be-missed destination is the Musée de la Chasse et de la Nature Dapper, a museum dedicated to promoting African and African diaspora cultures through contemporary art.

France's Countryside Charms:
Beyond the bustling cities, France's countryside holds remarkable art galleries and museums that often go unnoticed by mainstream tourists. In the picturesque region of Normandy, the Abbaye aux Hommes in Caen hosts a museum that takes visitors on a historical journey through the heart of this architectural masterpiece. In Provence, the Fondation Maeght showcases an impressive collection of modern and contemporary art amidst tranquil natural beauty.

Coastal Wonders:
France's coastal regions harbor hidden treasures for art enthusiasts seeking a unique experience. The Villa Noailles, nestled in the charming town of Hyères, transports visitors to the vibrant world of modern design, fashion, and photography. Embrace the picturesque beauty of the Mediterranean coast while exploring this lesser-known artistic gem. For those seeking a quieter coastal art retreat, the Musée Matisse in Le Cateau-Cambrésis, Normandy, presents a comprehensive exhibition dedicated to the life and work of Henri Matisse, one of the most influential artists of the 20th century.

Reimagining Industrial Heritage:
France's rich industrial history has yielded impressive art galleries and museums, which highlight the transformation of abandoned factories into artistic havens. In the northern city of Roubaix, La Piscine Museum invites visitors to explore an Art Deco swimming pool transformed into an exquisite display of fine arts, sculptures, and ceramics. In Lyon, the Musée des Confluences stands as a testament to the imagination of architects who have transformed an abandoned industrial wasteland into a stunning contemporary art space.

Unveiling Regional Treasures:

France's regional diversity is reflected in the artistic heritage showcased in smaller-scale museums and galleries. The Musée Fabre in Montpellier houses an astonishing collection of European art, from classical masters like Rubens and Courbet to modern visionaries. In Strasbourg, Museums-Palace Rohan beckons visitors to explore its three museums, which interweave art, history, and archaeology into a unique cultural experience.

As we conclude our exploration of these lesser-known art galleries and museums in France, we cannot help but feel a sense of awe and wonder at the depth and breadth of artistic offerings beyond the obvious choices. The hidden gems found on this journey provide an intimate, immersive, and distinctly individual experience that allows art lovers to engage with artistic masterpieces away from the crowds. These cultural treasures across France beckon both the seasoned traveler and the budding enthusiast to embark on a quest for hidden beauty, expanding horizons, and truly understanding the essence of French artistry.

Hidden artistic gems waiting to be explored

One out of reasons these artistic gems remain hidden is the dominance of mainstream art institutions and the commercial art market. Galleries and museums tend to focus on well-established artists or popular trends, leaving little space for emerging or unconventional talents. As a result, many gifted artists do not receive the recognition and opportunities they deserve to showcase their work. However, with the advent of social media and online platforms, there is newfound hope for these hidden gems to reach a wider audience. Artists can now showcase their creations on various online platforms and connect with art aficionados from around the world, providing a platform where their unique talents can truly shine.

Exploring these hidden artistic gems is not only a thrilling adventure but also an opportunity to expand our artistic horizons. Stepping away from the familiar names and celebrated masterpieces allows us to explore different styles, perspectives, and narratives that may be overlooked in traditional art circles. These hidden gems often challenge our preconceived notions of what art should be, encouraging us to question and re-evaluate our biases. Their works can ignite new passions, inspire us to take risks in our own artistic endeavors, and provide fresh and unconventional lenses through which we can perceive the world.

Furthermore, delving into hidden artistic gems can foster a sense of connection and empathy with the artists themselves. Unlike the well-known artists whose lives and works have been extensively documented, these hidden gems often maintain an air of mystery. Discovering their creations is akin to discovering a window into their souls – a glimpse into their thoughts, emotions, and personal journeys. It is an invitation to engage with their stories, motivations, and creative processes, forging a sense of intimacy and understanding. Exploring these hidden artistic gems allows us to become part of a shared narrative, creating a bridge between artist and audience that transcends time and space.

Despite their hidden status, many artistic gems hold immense value, both aesthetically and monetarily. In recent years, we have witnessed how the discovery of previously unknown artists' works has led to significant financial gains for collectors and investors. Moreover, investing in these hidden gems can be an opportunity to support and nurture artistic talent. By acquiring their works or amplifying their voices, we can contribute to their artistic journey and provide them with the recognition and opportunities they may have been denied otherwise. It is a chance to make a tangible and positive impact on the lives and careers of these talented artists whose work enriches our cultural landscape.

To unlock the true potential of these hidden artistic gems, it is crucial for art enthusiasts and scholars to actively seek them out and give them the attention they deserve. Engaging with lesser-known artists and their creations requires an open mind, a willingness to explore different artistic realms, and an appreciation for the diversity and beauty that exists beyond the mainstream. By actively supporting and promoting these talents, we can create a more inclusive and vibrant art world, one that recognizes that artistic excellence can be found in the unlikeliest of places. These lesser-known artists possess immense creativity and artistic merit, yet often go unnoticed within the dominant art institutions and commercial markets. Exploring these hidden gems not only expands our own artistic horizons but also nurtures and supports talented artists who deserve recognition and opportunities. By actively seeking out these hidden gems, we can contribute to a more inclusive and vibrant art world, one that celebrates the diversity and beauty that exists beyond the mainstream. So, let us embark on this exciting journey of exploration and discovery, and unveil the hidden artistic treasures that await us.

Chapter 7: Natural Beauty

Hidden natural wonders in the French landscape

France, known for its stunning architecture, rich history, and gastronomical delights, is also home to a plethora of hidden natural wonders. Beyond the bustling streets of Paris and the glamour of the French Riviera lie breathtaking landscapes that often go overlooked by tourists. From the rugged peaks of the Pyrenees to the mystical forests of the Ardennes, these hidden gems offer a captivating allure to those willing to explore off the beaten path. In this book, we aim to uncover some of these hidden natural wonders, shedding light on their unique features, ecological significance, and the experiences they offer to those who stumble upon them.

A component of most extraordinary natural wonders in France that often goes unnoticed is the Verdon Gorge. Nestled within the Provence-Alpes-Côte d'Azur region, this breathtaking ravine stretches for an astonishing 25 kilometers. Carved by the Verdon River over thousands of years, the gorge presents a mesmerizing display of turquoise waters winding through towering limestone cliffs. The Verdon Gorge offers an array of activities for outdoor enthusiasts, from kayaking and rock climbing to hiking along its scenic trails. Its diverse ecosystem is home to several rare bird species and a variety of flora, adding to its value as an ecological marvel.

In the south of France, the Camargue region presents yet another hidden natural wonder. This vast wetland, located at the mouth of the Rhône River, is known for its remarkable biodiversity and distinct landscapes. The Camargue is a haven for wildlife, boasting an impressive array of bird species, including the iconic pink flamingos that gather in flocks along its marshes. Horse lovers will be enchanted by the sight of the white Camargue horses galloping through the expansive plains, while nature enthusiasts can explore the unique salt marshes, dunes, and lagoons that shape this remarkable ecosystem. The Camargue not only offers a glimpse into France's natural beauty but also provides insights into the importance of wetland preservation.

Venturing further north, the French Alps reveal heavenly corners that astonish with their majesty. One such hidden gem is the Mercantour National Park, situated near the border with Italy. Spanning over 68,000 hectares, this mountainous wonderland is a paradise for hikers and nature lovers alike. Its snow-capped peaks, crystal-clear lakes, and picturesque alpine meadows attract visitors year-round. The Mercantour National Park houses an incredible array of wildlife, including ibex, chamois, and the rare European eagle owl. Its diverse flora is also a sight to behold, with vibrant wildflowers adorning the meadows during the summer months. Exploring this natural oasis provides not only a chance to connect with nature but also an opportunity to appreciate the preservation efforts undertaken to safeguard such extraordinary landscapes.

Heading towards the western part of France, the Ardennes

region presents an enchanting hidden wonder that captivates the imagination. This dense and mystical forest, often overshadowed by the allure of Paris, offers a tranquil escape from the modern world. The Ardennes Forest exudes an air of mystery, with its ancient oak trees, winding pathways, and hidden streams. Nature enthusiasts can immerse themselves in the peaceful ambiance, discover hidden waterfalls, and encounter wildlife such as deer, badgers, and even wild boars. The Ardennes also holds historical significance, being the site of important World War I battles, evoking a sense of reverence for the past amidst its natural beauty.

These hidden natural wonders in the French landscape are just a glimpse into the country's remarkable diversity and ecological richness. From breathtaking gorges to captivating wetlands, majestic mountains, and enchanting forests, France offers an abundance of hidden gems for those willing to venture off the beaten path. Exploring these natural wonders not only provides a deep connection with nature but also a sense of gratitude for the preservation efforts that protect these fragile ecosystems. So, grab your hiking boots, pack your bags, and embark on a journey to uncover the hidden natural wonders of the French landscape.

Off-the-beaten-path spots for nature enthusiasts

One off-the-beaten-path destination that should be on every nature enthusiast's list is the Snaefellsnes Peninsula in Iceland. This picturesque peninsula offers a diverse array of landscapes, ranging from volcanic peaks to black sand beaches. With its remote location, Snaefellsnes is a haven for wildlife, making it an ideal spot for birdwatching and marine life observation. The iconic Snaefellsjokull volcano, famous for its association with Jules Verne's "Journey to the Center of the Earth," serves as a stunning backdrop to the peninsula. Hiking trails stretch across the rugged terrain, enabling adventurous souls to explore the unique flora and fauna. For those seeking tranquility and awe-inspiring natural beauty, the Snaefellsnes Peninsula is a must-visit destination.

Another hidden gem for nature enthusiasts is the Simien Mountains National Park in Ethiopia. Known as the "Roof of Africa," this majestic mountain range offers unparalleled scenery and breathtaking hikes. The rugged peaks, deep valleys, and sheer cliffs create a dramatic landscape that stirs the soul. As one explores the vast network of trails, they may encounter rare and endemic wildlife species, including the Ethiopian wolf and the endangered Walia ibex. The park is also home to numerous bird species and provides a perfect backdrop for photography enthusiasts. For those seeking an off-the-beaten-path adventure that combines awe-inspiring landscapes with unique wildlife encounters, the Simien Mountains National Park is an absolute treasure.

For nature enthusiasts longing for an off-the-beaten-path beach destination, the Palomino Coast in Colombia is an ideal choice. Nestled between the tranquil Caribbean Sea and the lush rainforest-covered Sierra Nevada Mountains, Palomino offers a serene escape from the typical tourist hubs. Its pristine beaches, dotted with swaying palm trees and turquoise waters, provide the perfect setting for relaxation and tranquility. The nearby Cocora Valley, famous for its towering wax palm trees, adds another layer of natural beauty to this already enchanting destination. Palomino also offers opportunities for river tubing, hiking, and exploring indigenous communities, truly immersing visitors in the local culture and natural wonders of the region.

One cannot discuss off-the-beaten-path spots for nature enthusiasts without mentioning Bialowieza Forest in Poland and Belarus. This ancient primeval forest, a UNESCO World Heritage site, is one of the last and largest remaining parts of the immense primeval forest that once covered much of Europe. Bialowieza Forest is home to the European bison, the continent's heaviest land animal, as well as numerous other rare and endangered species. Exploring the forest's network of trails, visitors will feel transported back in time, surrounded by towering trees and enchanting wildlife. The forest also offers a unique opportunity for nature enthusiasts to learn about and support conservation efforts, ensuring the preservation of this invaluable natural treasure.

Off-the-beaten-path spots for nature enthusiasts provide a gateway to unforgettable experiences and a deeper appreciation for the natural world. Whether venturing into the remote landscapes of Iceland's Snaefellsnes Peninsula, exploring the dramatic beauty of Ethiopia's Simien Mountains, lounging on the serene beaches of Colombia's Palomino Coast, or immersing in the ancient magnificence of Bialowieza Forest, these hidden gems offer a chance to escape the crowds and embrace the splendor of nature. For those seeking a one-of-a-kind adventure and an opportunity to create lasting memories, these off-the-beaten-path spots are an absolute must-explore. So pack your backpack, lace up your hiking boots, and embark on a journey of discovery into the heart of nature's hidden treasures.

Chapter 8: Châteaux and Castles

Exploring lesser-known châteaux and castles in France

France is renowned for its numerous châteaux and castles, which ignite the imagination with their rich history and architectural marvels. While iconic destinations like the Palace of Versailles and Château de Chambord often steal the spotlight, there exists a treasure trove of lesser-known châteaux and castles that offer a unique and enchanting experience for those willing to venture off the beaten path. In this book, we will explore some of these hidden gems, showcasing their allure and inviting travelers to embark on a journey of discovery through the lesser-known castles and châteaux of France.

Our exploration begins with the picturesque region of Normandy, nestled in the northwestern part of France. Here, amidst charming countryside and coastal landscapes, lies the Château Gaillard. Constructed under the command of Richard the Lionheart, this medieval fortress stands proudly atop a hill overlooking the Seine River. With its imposing stone walls and strategic location, the Château Gaillard offers a glimpse into the military history of France. Visitors can stroll through the ruins and imagine the battles and sieges that once unfolded within these very walls, marveling at the architectural prowess of its time.

Moving eastward, we arrive in the beautiful region of Burgundy, renowned for its world-class wines and scenic landscapes. It is within this region that we uncover the hidden gem that is the Château de Cormatin. Built in the early 17th century, this grand residence embodies the elegance and opulence of the French Renaissance. Its serene gardens, adorned with intricate mazes and vibrant flower beds, provide a tranquil retreat for visitors seeking respite from the bustling city life. As one explores the lavish interior, they will find themselves transported back in time, relishing in the extravagant lifestyle of the French nobility.

Continuing our journey, we find ourselves in the idyllic Loire Valley, often referred to as the "Garden of France" due to its abundance of charming castles and châteaux. While the region boasts famous landmarks like Chenonceau and Amboise, we turn our attention to the lesser-known gem of the Château d'Azay-le-Rideau. Nestled on the banks of the Indre River, this fairy-tale castle emanates elegance and romance. With its delicate turrets, pristine white stone, and surrounding moat, the Château d'Azay-le-Rideau captures the imagination, reflecting the harmonious blend of French Renaissance and early French Classicism. Visitors can explore its splendidly furnished rooms, envisioning the lives of the nobility who once called this enchanting place home.

Our journey would not be complete without a visit to the region of Provence, renowned for its vibrant colors, fragrant lavender fields, and rich cultural heritage. Here, tucked away in the Luberon Mountains, lies the Château de Lacoste. Surrounded by lush gardens and vineyards, this fortified castle reflects the medieval architecture of the region, with its sturdy stone walls and tower-like structures. Beyond its historical charm, the Château de Lacoste is also a hub for contemporary art, hosting exhibitions and events that showcase the intersection of tradition and modernity. Visitors can immerse themselves in the cultural offerings while basking in the serene beauty of the Provençal countryside.

As we conclude our exploration of the lesser-known châteaux and castles in France, it becomes evident that these hidden gems hold a charm and allure that is often eclipsed by their more famous counterparts. From the military fortresses of Normandy to the elegant residences of Burgundy and the fairytale castles of the Loire Valley, each château and castle provides a unique glimpse into the rich history and cultural heritage of France. By venturing off the beaten path and embarking on a journey to discover these hidden treasures, travelers can experience the true depth and diversity of the French architectural and historical landscape. So, let us set forth on this journey of exploration, guided by curiosity and a desire to uncover the enchanting tales held within the lesser-known châteaux and castles of France.

Hidden architectural treasures in the French countryside

One such remarkable architectural treasure is the Chateau de Chenonceau, known as the "Ladies' Castle," which spans the Cher River in the Loire Valley. Built in the early 16th century, this majestic castle boasts a unique design that incorporates both Gothic and Renaissance elements. Its gallery, which stretches across the river, is adorned with elegant arches and surrounded by manicured gardens, adding to its ethereal beauty. As one wanders through its opulent rooms and meticulously manicured gardens, it becomes apparent why Chenonceau has captured the imagination of countless visitors seeking a glimpse into the opulence of French history.

Another hidden gem is the Abbey of Fontenay, located in the Burgundy region. Founded in 1118, this incredibly preserved medieval abbey showcases the simple yet elegant Cistercian architectural style. The tranquil surroundings of Fontenay allow visitors to immerse themselves in the peaceful atmosphere that the monks once experienced. From the abbey church with its impressive soaring vaults to the beautiful gardens and serene ponds, Fontenay is a testament to the enduring beauty and spirituality of medieval architecture.

Moving further south, the fortified city of Carcassonne in the Languedoc-Roussillon region is a magnificent example of medieval military architecture. Its imposing double walls, watchtowers, and drawbridges transport visitors back in time to the era of knights and sieges. The intricate details of Carcassonne's fortifications, including the Basilique Saint-Nazaire and the Chateau Comtal, offer insight into the strategic importance of this fortress city throughout history. Its well-preserved medieval streets and charming squares further add to the allure of this hidden architectural treasure.

Beyond castles and fortresses, France also offers a wealth of charming manor houses that are scattered throughout the countryside. These elegant residences, often surrounded by beautifully manicured gardens, offer an intimate glimpse into French rural life over the centuries. From the grand Chateau de Villandry in the Loire Valley, known for its meticulously designed

Renaissance gardens, to the charming Chateau de Gudanes in the Pyrenees, which is currently undergoing a passionate restoration, these manor houses showcase the architectural diversity and captivating stories of their past occupants.

While these architectural treasures may be hidden away in the French countryside, they are not to be overlooked. These masterpieces not only exemplify the architectural prowess of their time but also provide a profound understanding of France's rich cultural and historical heritage. Whether admiring the grandeur of a castle, exploring the serenity of an abbey, or meandering through the elegant rooms of a manor house, each hidden treasure holds its own unique allure, waiting to be discovered and appreciated by those who seek to immerse themselves in the beauty of the French countryside.

Chapter 9: Quaint Villages

Discovering charming villages off the tourist trail

One in a group of most alluring aspects of discovering off-the-beaten-path villages is the opportunity to witness untouched architectural wonders. These villages often boast historic buildings and houses that have preserved their original charm, showcasing a rich history that is often absent from more touristy areas. Walking through the cobbled streets of these villages, one can admire the intricate details and unique characteristics of the architecture. From cottages with thatched roofs to colorful facades and ornate doorways, every building tells a story, adding to the village's allure. The absence of mass tourism allows for a more immersive experience, enabling travelers to explore these architectural marvels at their own pace, appreciating their authenticity and intricacy.

In addition to their architectural treasures, hidden villages also offer breathtaking landscapes that are often overlooked by guidebooks and travel agencies. Nestled amidst rolling hills, verdant valleys, or winding rivers, these villages provide a peaceful haven away from the hustle and bustle of popular tourist destinations. Picture-perfect countryside scenes unfold at every turn, showcasing the unspoiled beauty of nature. Trails wind through idyllic meadows, leading to breathtaking viewpoints where visitors can revel in the splendor of panoramic vistas. The tranquility of these landscapes can be truly rejuvenating, offering an escape from the stresses of everyday life and providing a chance to reconnect with nature in its purest form.

What truly sets these charming villages apart, however, is the warm hospitality and genuine connections that can be forged with the locals. Away from the crowds, residents of these villages often have more time and inclination to engage with visitors. This may involve sharing stories and local folklore, imparting wisdom about age-old traditions, or simply offering a friendly smile and warm welcome. By interacting with the locals, travelers can gain unique insights into the cultural fabric of the area, fostering a deeper understanding and appreciation for the destination. Through genuine connections, friendships can be formed, allowing for an authentic experience that cannot be replicated in more touristy locales.

Discovering charming villages off the tourist trail requires a sense of adventure and a willingness to step outside one's comfort zone. However, the rewards that await those who embark on this journey are invaluable. From architectural wonders that whisper tales of the past to awe-inspiring landscapes that invite contemplation and reflection, these hidden gems offer a glimpse into a world less explored. The chance to interact with locals, learn from their traditions, and share in their warm hospitality adds an authentic touch to the travel experience. So, next time you plan a trip, consider straying off the beaten path and uncovering the secrets of these charming villages. You will not only discover hidden treasures but also create memories that will stay with you forever.

Local traditions and customs in lesser-known villages

In the heart of Rajasthan, a state in western India known for its royal history and breathtaking architecture, lies the little-known village of Mandawa. This quaint settlement, with its narrow streets lined with exquisitely painted havelis (traditional mansions), offers a glimpse into the region's vibrant past. The locals here are deeply connected to their roots and proudly showcase their traditional Rajasthani customs.

A component of most prominent traditions in Mandawa is the celebration of Teej, a colorful festival dedicated to the Goddess Parvati. On this day, married women dress in vibrant traditional attire and come together to offer prayers and sing traditional songs. The streets are adorned with artistic patterns created from colored powders, and the mesmerizing sound of folk music fills the air. This lively festival not only showcases the rich culture of the village but also fosters a sense of unity among its inhabitants.

Heading to the far east, we arrive at the secluded village of Shirakawa-go in Japan. Tucked away in the breathtaking Japanese Alps, Shirakawa-go is home to the unique Gassho-zukuri-style farmhouses. These classical structures, with their steep thatched roofs resembling the shape of praying hands, are a testament to the architectural ingenuity of the locals. The village proudly treasures this heritage and offers visitors the opportunity to experience the joys of farm life through hands-on activities and cultural exchanges.

One of the most cherished customs in Shirakawa-go is the Obon Festival, a celebration honoring ancestors. During this festival, locals light delicate paper lanterns and release them into the river, creating a mesmerizing spectacle of floating lights. Traditional dances and music accompany this heartfelt commemoration, bringing together generations to express their gratitude and love for those who came before them. The Obon Festival is a poignant reminder of the village's deep-rooted traditions, fostering a profound sense of community and continuity.

Turning our attention to South America, we find ourselves mesmerized by the lesser-known village of Ollantaytambo in the Sacred Valley of the Incas, Peru. Ollantaytambo, boasting its ancient stone terraces and impressive Incan ruins, is a living testament to the grandeur and advanced engineering of the Inca civilization. It is a place where time seems to stand still, and the local customs continue to thrive.

One such custom is the Inti Raymi festival, a celebration of the sun god Inti, which takes place on the winter solstice. Thousands of locals dressed in colorful traditional attire gather in the main plaza to witness ancient rituals and traditional dances that pay homage to their Inca ancestors. The festival, with its vibrant energy and dynamic performances, encapsulates the profound connection between the people of Ollantaytambo and their rich heritage. It offers visitors not only a glimpse into the history of the village but also a chance to be part of a living cultural experience. These communities, tucked away from the limelight, hold onto their customs with pride and dedication, providing an opportunity for travelers to immerse themselves in authentic experiences. Whether it is the vibrant Teej festival in Mandawa, the heartfelt Obon Festival in Shirakawa-go, or the ancient Inti Raymi celebration in Ollantaytambo, these customs reflect the unwavering spirit of the locals and their desire to preserve their cultural legacies. By venturing off the beaten path and embracing these lesser-known villages, we can unlock the secrets of their traditions and gain a deeper understanding of the world we inhabit.

Chapter 10: Rural Retreats

Hidden gems for a peaceful countryside retreat

Amidst the chaos of urban life, a countryside retreat offers a peaceful escape to restore and rejuvenate the soul. While popular tourist destinations are often crowded and bustling, hidden gems in the countryside provide a unique and serene atmosphere. In this article, we will explore some of these hidden gems, highlighting their distinct features and the tranquility they offer to those seeking a countryside retreat.

1. The Enchanting Lake District:
Nestled in the north-west region of England, the Lake District is renowned for its breathtaking landscapes and a peaceful ambiance that makes it an ideal retreat for nature lovers. The region's pristine lakes, picturesque mountains, and charming villages create a sense of tranquility and serenity. Away from the hustle and bustle of urban life, visitors can embark on scenic walks, boat rides, or simply sit beside a shimmering lake, allowing the soothing sounds of nature to wash over them. Whether it's exploring the famous trails such as Wastwater or immersing oneself in the literary heritage of William Wordsworth and Beatrix Potter, the Lake District offers a hidden gem for those seeking a peaceful countryside retreat.

2. The Tranquil Villages of Tuscany:
Italy's Tuscany region is world-famous for its stunning landscapes, vineyards, and historic cities. However, nestled among the rolling hills and vine-clad countryside, lies a collection of small, picturesque villages that offer a peaceful haven far from the tourist crowds. Places like Volterra, Montepulciano, and San Gimignano showcase medieval architecture, charming cobbled streets, and breathtaking vistas. These hidden gems allow visitors to immerse themselves in the slow-paced lifestyle of the countryside, savoring delicious local cuisine, exploring local vineyards, or simply basking in the warm Italian sun. A countryside retreat in Tuscany's tranquil villages promises an escape from the chaotic city life, providing a peaceful setting to unwind and recharge.

3. The Serene Scottish Highlands:
For those seeking solitude and majestic landscapes, the Scottish Highlands offers an idyllic countryside retreat. With its rugged mountains, shimmering lochs, and vast expanses of unspoiled wilderness, this hidden gem of Scotland attracts travelers seeking peace and tranquility. Visitors can explore the legendary Loch Ness, hike through the Cairngorms National Park, or simply soak in the silence while surrounded by breathtaking panoramas. The Highlands offer a unique blend of mystery, beauty, and seclusion, making it a perfect destination for a countryside retreat that allows one to reconnect with nature and find inner calm.

4. The Tranquility of New Zealand's South Island:
New Zealand's South Island is a treasure trove of hidden gems for those longing for a peaceful countryside retreat. With its diverse landscapes ranging from snow-capped mountains to

pristine lakes and golden beaches, this island offers an array of secluded spots. The Southern Alps provide a serene backdrop, where visitors can enjoy hiking, skiing, or simply immersing themselves in the silence of nature. The Milford Sound, with its majestic fjords, offers a truly awe-inspiring setting for a peaceful escape, surrounded by untouched wilderness. The South Island's tranquil beauty and serene atmosphere make it a hidden gem for those seeking a countryside retreat away from the chaos of everyday life.

In the quest for tranquility, hidden gems in the countryside provide a refuge from the noise and stress of modern life. The Lake District, Tuscany's villages, the Scottish Highlands, and New Zealand's South Island all offer peaceful countryside retreats amidst stunning natural landscapes. Whether it is through serene walks by shimmering lakes, exploring charming villages, hiking through majestic mountains, or simply absorbing the silence, these hidden gems provide the perfect setting to recharge and find inner peace. So, take a break from life's chaos, venture beyond the well-known tourist destinations, and discover these hidden gems for a truly peaceful countryside retreat.

Unique accommodations in lesser-known rural areas

One type of unique accommodation that can be found in lesser-known rural areas is the traditional farmhouse. Tucked away in scenic countryside, these farmhouses provide a distinct and charming setting for travelers seeking a peaceful escape from the busyness of everyday life. With their rustic, yet elegant interiors and stunning views of rolling hills or meadows, staying in a traditional farmhouse gives visitors a chance to experience the authentic rural lifestyle. From waking up to the sounds of chirping birds and grazing farm animals to enjoying home-cooked meals made with locally sourced ingredients, every moment spent in a farmhouse offers a glimpse into the rich agricultural heritage of the region.

In addition to farmhouses, another unique accommodation option in lesser-known rural areas is the eco-lodge. These sustainable and environmentally-friendly lodgings are often nestled within lush forests, near pristine rivers, or on the outskirts of nature reserves. Constructed using locally sourced materials and built with minimal ecological impact, eco-lodges strive to maintain harmony with the surrounding environment. Guests can unwind in cozy cabins or spacious yurts, all while being surrounded by the beauty of nature. Many eco-lodges also offer activities such as guided hikes, wildlife spotting, and nature walks, providing visitors with the opportunity to connect with the natural wonders that abound in these rural areas.

For travelers seeking a truly unique experience, staying in a converted historical building can be an extraordinary choice. Lesser-known rural areas often have hidden treasures in the form of old castles, charming windmills, or traditional village houses that have been transformed into accommodations. These restored buildings not only provide a glimpse into the cultural and historical significance of the region but also offer a sense of nostalgia and authenticity. Whether it's spending the night in a medieval fortress or a centuries-old stone cottage, these converted historical buildings allow visitors to step back in time and appreciate the architectural beauty and craftsmanship of a bygone era.

In addition to the accommodation options mentioned above, glamping has become increasingly popular in lesser-known rural areas. Combining the luxuries of a hotel stay with the beauty of the outdoors, glamping offers a unique and unforgettable experience. Far from the traditional concept of camping, glamping allows travelers to enjoy the beauty of nature without compromising on comfort. Whether it's a luxurious tent on a remote hillside, a treehouse nestled among the treetops, or a cozy cabin with panoramic views, glamping accommodations offer a blend of luxury and ruggedness. From star-gazing under clear skies to waking up to breathtaking sunrise views, glamping in rural areas provides a magical experience that is sure to leave a lasting impression. These hidden gems provide an opportunity for travelers to delve into the local culture, soak in the natural beauty, and experience a unique way of life. With a plethora of unique accommodations to choose from, such as traditional farmhouses, eco-lodges, converted historical buildings, and glamping sites, staying in these rural areas becomes an adventure in itself. Whether you seek tranquility, connection with nature, or a taste of history, the accommodations in lesser-known rural areas are sure to provide an extraordinary experience that will leave you with lasting memories.

Chapter 11: Secret Gardens

Unveiling hidden gardens and parks in France

Nestled away from the bustling city streets and the clamor of tourists, these enchanting oases offer a serene escape, where nature gracefully intertwines with human artistry. In this exploration, we will take a closer look at some of these hidden gems, exploring their origins, unique features, and cultural significance, inviting you to embark on a journey through the secret gardens and parks that lie nestled within the French countryside.

The Hidden Gardens of Château de Villandry:

Nestled within the heart of the Loire Valley, the Château de Villandry boasts more than just its opulent architecture; it is home to one of France's most enchanting hidden gardens. Stepping through the entrance, one is transported back in time, as meticulously manicured paths wind through symmetrical flowerbeds and intricate topiary designs. This Renaissance masterpiece displays the grandeur of love, water, music, and gardens, each garden representing an essential element of human existence. The ornamental vegetable garden, the pièce de résistance, is a true marvel, not only serving as an aesthetic delight but also providing inspiration for modern-day kitchen gardens around the world.

The Secret Gardens of Versailles:

While Versailles is well-known for its grand palace and sprawling gardens, it harbors a secret that is often overlooked by the masses. Behind regal hedges and hidden gates lie the captivating secret gardens of this magnificent historical site. Originally designed for the pleasure of Louis XIV, these secluded gardens carry an air of intimacy, inviting guests to stroll through lush greenery, vibrant flower beds, and tranquil fountains. With their hidden charms, these secret gardens provide respite from the crowds, allowing visitors to immerse themselves in the natural beauty that surrounds this iconic palace.

Exploring the Hidden Parks of Paris:

Paris, the City of Lights, is not only famous for its iconic landmarks but also for its hidden parks that invite moments of tranquility amid the urban chaos. Beyond the well-trodden paths of gardens like Luxembourg and Tuileries, lesser-known parks dot the city, patiently waiting to be discovered. Parc Monceau, once a private garden of the Duke of Chartres, is now open to the public, offering a whimsical landscape adorned with statues, follies, and romantic bridges. Parc des Buttes-Chaumont, with its hilly terrain and glistening lake, provides a serene escape from the bustling city streets. These hidden parks offer glimpses into the different epochs of Parisian history, each with its unique charm and stories to tell.

Preserving the Hidden Gardens and Parks of France:

As we unveil the splendor of France's hidden gardens and parks, it is crucial to acknowledge the importance of their preservation. These secret oases are not only a testament to the country's rich heritage but also to the tireless efforts of dedicated gardeners and conservationists. With increasing urbanization and environmental challenges, it is essential to protect these serene spaces, ensuring their beauty can be enjoyed by future generations. By fostering public awareness and supporting initiatives that promote the preservation and restoration of these hidden treasures, we can play a part in safeguarding France's natural and cultural heritage.

Unveiling the hidden gardens and parks of France allows us to shift our focus from the famous landmarks and bustling cityscapes, offering insight into the country's more tranquil and untouched side. These secret spaces not only showcase the French art of gardening but also connect us with the nation's history, culture, and spirituality. Through the footsteps of countless visitors who have marveled at their beauty, these hidden gardens and parks have evolved into time capsules, awaiting discovery by those who seek solace and inspiration in their verdant corners. So, whether you find yourself exploring the grandeur of the Château de Villandry, exploring the secrets of Versailles, or seeking respite in the pockets of peace within Paris, immerse yourself in the beauty that lies within France's hidden gardens and parks, and let the magic unfold.

Serene spots for relaxation and reflection

One such serene spot is the stunningly beautiful Japanese Zen garden in Kyoto, Japan. Known for its meticulously designed landscapes and emphasis on balance and harmony, these gardens offer a serene and contemplative atmosphere. As you walk along the carefully arranged paths, surrounded by meticulously pruned trees, carefully placed stones, and tranquil water features, you cannot help but feel a sense of calm wash over you. The simplicity of the design allows for clear and focused thinking, making it an ideal location for meditation and self-reflection. The sounds of flowing water and the gentle rustling of leaves create a soothing ambience that envelops you, melting away any stress or worry. Visiting a Zen garden in Kyoto can be an immersive experience, transporting you to a place of peace and serenity.

If you prefer a more natural setting, the Amazon Rainforest in Brazil offers unparalleled beauty and tranquility. As you explore the dense foliage and listen to the symphony of birds and insects, you are enveloped in a sense of awe and wonder. The sheer size and diversity of plant and animal life in the rainforest leave you humbled and remind you of the interconnectedness of all living things. Finding a secluded spot within the rainforest, perhaps near a clear stream or a hidden waterfall, allows for uninterrupted introspection and reflection. Surrounded by the gentle sounds of nature and the vibrant colors of the flora, you can let go of the outside world and focus on your inner thoughts and emotions. The Amazon Rainforest offers a serene escape from civilization, allowing you to reconnect with the natural world and find solace in its beauty.

Closer to home, the peaceful and picturesque Amalfi Coast in Italy provides a serene spot for relaxation and reflection. Nestled between dramatic cliffs and the sparkling blue waters of the Mediterranean Sea, this coastal paradise exudes tranquility and charm. The slow-paced lifestyle and warm hospitality of the locals create an inviting atmosphere, making it a perfect spot to unwind and reflect on life's joys and challenges. You can take leisurely walks along the coastal paths, breathing in the fresh sea air and taking in the breathtaking views. Finding a cozy café or restaurant overlooking the sea allows for moments of quiet contemplation while indulging in delicious Italian cuisine. The Amalfi Coast offers a blend of natural beauty, cultural richness, and a sense of tranquility that makes it an ideal destination for relaxation and self-reflection.

For a more secluded and introspective experience, the Tibetan monasteries nestled in the Himalayas offer a unique opportunity for reflection and inner exploration. These spiritual havens are located in remote mountainous regions, away from the distractions of modern life. As you ascend through winding paths and valleys surrounded by majestic mountains, you can feel your worries and stresses melting away. The monasteries themselves are sanctuaries of peace, with their intricate artwork, colorful prayer flags, and serene meditation halls. Engaging in mindfulness practices alongside Buddhist monks allows you to delve deeper into your own spiritual journey. The solitude of the mountains encourages introspection, as you contemplate the vastness of the universe and your place within it. The Tibetan monasteries offer an immersive and transformative experience, allowing you to connect with your inner self in a way that is truly profound. Whether in a meticulously designed Japanese Zen garden, the untamed beauty of the Amazon Rainforest, the idyllic Amalfi Coast, or the secluded Tibetan monasteries, these places allow us to step away from the noise and find solace in nature, culture, and our own thoughts. By seeking out these serene spots, we can embark on a journey of self-discovery, gaining insight, peace, and clarity in our lives. So, embrace the opportunity to escape to these serene havens and let them nurture your body, mind, and soul.

Chapter 12: Specialty Markets

Hidden markets offering unique products and local foods

A member of most alluring aspects of hidden markets is the array of unique products they offer. These markets provide a platform for artisans and craftsmen to showcase their skills and produce handcrafted items that are a true testament to the rich heritage and traditions of a particular region. From intricately woven textiles and pottery adorned with intricate motifs to fine jewelry and leather goods crafted with meticulous precision, hidden markets present an exquisite range of products that cannot be replicated by mass-produced alternatives. Each item tells a story, reflecting the intimate connection between artisans and their craft, and offering consumers a chance to own a piece of living history.

In addition to the remarkable array of handicrafts, hidden markets are also veritable treasure troves of local and traditional foods. These markets offer an invaluable opportunity to taste and savor the unique flavors and culinary traditions of a specific region. Farmers, growers, and small-scale producers come together at hidden markets to showcase an abundance of seasonal fruits, vegetables, and herbs that are not readily available in mainstream outlets. The flavors are often intensively concentrated due to the care and attention devoted to cultivating these items in small batches, resulting in a taste experience that is unparalleled. Furthermore, hidden markets frequently feature traditional dishes prepared by local chefs, providing an authentic and immersive culinary experience for visitors.

Hidden markets have a cultural significance that extends beyond their exceptional products and local foods. They act as vibrant hubs that foster community cohesion, preserve traditional knowledge, and celebrate cultural diversity. These markets provide a platform for artisans, farmers, and producers to connect with their customers on a personal level, sharing the stories behind their products and forging meaningful relationships. By patronizing hidden markets, consumers not only support the livelihoods of these hardworking individuals but also contribute to the preservation of cultural heritage. In a time when global mass production threatens to homogenize our cultural landscapes, hidden markets serve as vital spaces that honor and celebrate local traditions, ensuring their continuity for future generations.

Recent years have witnessed a growing interest among consumers in supporting hidden markets and seeking out unique products and local foods. This shift can be attributed to a number of factors, including the rise of conscious consumerism, a desire for authentic experiences, and an increased appreciation for the craftsmanship inherent in handmade and locally produced goods. As individuals become more aware of the environmental and social implications of their purchasing decisions, they are actively seeking alternatives that align with their values. Hidden markets, with their emphasis on sustainability, traceability, and supporting local economies, perfectly fit these criteria. These markets provide an opportunity to delve into the cultural tapestry of a region, offering a glimpse into the lives and traditions of artisans, farmers, and producers. Through showcasing distinctive handicrafts, a plethora of local foods, and fostering community cohesion, hidden markets hold immense cultural significance. They also serve as a beacon for conscious consumers looking to support sustainable practices and seek out authentic, high-quality products. As we embark on this journey through the hidden markets of the world, let us celebrate the creativity, diversity, and traditions that these markets encapsulate, and embrace the opportunity to be part of a movement that values uniqueness, sustainability, and local communities.

Shopping experiences off the tourist radar

One effective way to discover shopping experiences off the tourist radar is to explore less-popular neighborhoods or districts within a city. While major commercial areas may be bustling with activity, they often contain internationally recognized chain stores and brands. By venturing further afield, you are likely to stumble upon local markets, family-owned boutiques, and emerging designers showcasing their unique creations. These hidden gems can provide a refreshing alternative to the mainstream shopping experience, providing access to products that are not commonly found in popular shopping districts.

It is also worth mentioning the significance of local markets in offering an authentic shopping experience. Farmers' markets, flea markets, and bazaars can be found in many cities around the world and are usually frequented by locals seeking fresh produce, unique crafts, and handmade products. These markets can be an excellent opportunity to interact with vendors and artisans, gain insights into the local culture, and support small-scale businesses. While the wares may vary depending on the location, you are likely to find a wide array of goods such as local delicacies, traditional textiles, handmade jewelry, and unique souvenirs.

Another avenue to explore when seeking shopping experiences off the tourist radar is to engage with local communities through cultural events and festivals. These celebrations often showcase the traditions, customs, and artistic skills of a particular region or country. Many cultural events include marketplaces or stalls where local artisans and craftsmen sell their products. This can be an incredible opportunity to witness traditional craftsmanship up close and even learn from masters of their trade. By attending these events, you not only support local businesses but also gain a deeper understanding of the local culture and traditions.

In recent years, the rise of social media and online platforms has made it easier to discover unique shopping experiences off the tourist radar. Many cities now have dedicated websites or social media accounts that highlight lesser-known shops, markets, and designers. These platforms provide a wealth of information and insider tips on where to find hidden shopping gems. Additionally, travelers themselves have become influential content creators, sharing their experiences and recommendations through blogs, vlogs, and social media posts. When researching your destination, be sure to tap into these resources to identify hidden shopping areas and gain insights from fellow travelers who have explored off-the-beaten-path locations.

To fully enjoy and make the most of your shopping experiences off the tourist radar, it is essential to approach them with an open mind and a willingness to embrace the local culture. Engage with shop owners and vendors, ask them about their products, and show genuine interest in their craftsmanship. You may discover fascinating stories behind the products and forge connections with the people who create them. Remember, shopping is not just about acquiring goods; it is also about immersing yourself in the local culture, fostering connections, and contributing to the sustainability of the local economy. By venturing into less-explored neighborhoods, visiting local markets and cultural events, and utilizing online resources, you can uncover hidden shopping gems that provide an enriching and personalized experience. Take the time to engage with locals, learn about their craft, and support small businesses to contribute meaningfully to the local economy and create lasting memories of your journey.

Chapter 13: Literary Landmarks

Lesser-known places of literary significance in France

One such hidden treasure is the coastal town of Honfleur in Normandy. While primarily known for its charming harbor and picturesque streets, Honfleur holds a literary significance that is often overshadowed by its natural beauty. This quaint town was home to celebrated French poet Charles Baudelaire during his exile from Paris. Baudelaire's time in Honfleur inspired some of his most influential and infamous works, notably "Les Fleurs du Mal" (The Flowers of Evil). Literary pilgrims can stroll along the cobbled streets, marvel at the same landscapes that captivated Baudelaire's imagination, and perhaps even find inspiration for their own artistic endeavors.

Another hidden gem is the village of Illiers-Combray, located in the heart of the Loire Valley. While the name may not ring a bell for most, this unassuming village holds great importance for literature aficionados. Illiers-Combray served as the inspiration for Marcel Proust's fictional town of Combray in his monumental work, "In Search of Lost Time." Proust vividly depicted the landscapes, landmarks, and people of Illiers-Combray within his novel, immortalizing the village within the realms of literature. Visitors can explore the village, taking in the sights that inspired Proust's prose and perhaps even relive their own personal memories while meandering through the streets of Illiers-Combray.

Moving further south, the charming town of Céret in the Pyrénées-Orientales region also holds its own literary secrets. Céret was the home of esteemed Irish playwright and novelist, Samuel Beckett, during his self-imposed exile from Britain. While residing in Céret, Beckett worked on his groundbreaking play, "Waiting for Godot," which would later become a seminal work within the realm of theater. Literary enthusiasts can visit the house where Beckett once lived, now transformed into the Samuel Beckett Cultural Center, and explore the museum dedicated to his life and work. The surrounding landscapes of Céret, with their breathtaking beauty and tranquility, offer the perfect setting for contemplation and reflection, drawing visitors into the same creative space that Beckett once occupied.

Continuing our literary journey across France, we come to the region of Champagne-Ardenne, where the picturesque village of Essoyes awaits. This unassuming village played a significant role in the life and works of French Impressionist painter Pierre-Auguste Renoir. Renoir spent many summers in Essoyes, captivated by the enchanting landscapes and the peaceful atmosphere that permeated the village. It was during his time in Essoyes that he painted some of his most exquisite masterpieces, often featuring the serene countryside and the local residents, who became his muses. Visitors can immerse themselves in the rustic charm of the village, walk in Renoir's footsteps, and gain a deeper understanding of the connection between literature and art.

Lastly, the enchanting island of Belle-île-en-Mer, situated off the coast of Brittany, provides another lesser-known literary haven. This idyllic island served as the inspiration for French author Sarah Bernhardt's semi-autobiographical novel, "Petite Idole." Bernhardt, celebrated for both her acting and writing, found solace and inspiration on Belle-île-en-Mer, drawing upon the beauty and isolation of the island for her novel. Visitors can explore the rugged coastline, discover hidden coves, and imagine themselves within the pages of Bernhardt's book, embracing the creative energy that flows through the island. These hidden gems offer an opportunity for literary enthusiasts to delve into the country's rich literary heritage and gain a deeper understanding of the creative process behind renowned works. From the coastal town of Honfleur, to the village of Illiers-Combray, the town of Céret, the village of Essoyes, and the island of Belle-île-en-Mer, these lesser-known places in France provide an invaluable experience for those seeking to explore the literary landscapes and stories that continue to shape the country's cultural identity.

Hidden spots for book lovers to explore

While well-known bookstores and libraries often come to mind, there are numerous hidden spots around the world that offer unique experiences for those seeking solace among the pages. From diminutive, tucked-away bookshops to literary-themed cafes and secret libraries, these hidden gems can transport bibliophiles to enchanting realms of imagination and knowledge. In this article, we will take an exhilarating journey through some of these remarkable places, where bookworms can revel in the magic of literature.

Charming Book Nooks and Independent Stores:

One in a group of delights of being a book aficionado is stumbling upon quaint book nooks and independent stores bursting with character. Tucked away on narrow streets or nestled in forgotten corners of cities, these hidden gems offer respite from the hustle and bustle of modern life. In Dublin, Ireland, for instance, the Secret Book and Record Store beckons visitors into a delightfully cluttered space where books of all genres are stacked haphazardly, waiting to be discovered. Similarly, in Edinburgh, Scotland, the Armchair Books provides a cozy escape into a labyrinthine world of books, with every crevice filled to the brim with literary treasures. These hidden spots not only offer unique finds but also inspire the joy of serendipitous encounters with literature.

Literary Cafes:
Imagine savoring a cup of steaming tea or coffee while losing yourself in the lines of a favorite novel. Literary cafes provide bookworms with the perfect ambience to do just that. Often adorned with shelves upon shelves of books and exuding a tranquil atmosphere, these places allow visitors to engage with literature while indulging in delectable treats. In Paris, France, Shakespeare and Company Cafe invites readers to bask in the legacy of famous literary figures who once frequented the legendary bookstore next door. In London, the Book Club Cafe in Shoreditch offers a haven where visitors can peruse books, engage in literary discussions, and enjoy live events. These welcoming literary cafes provide spaces for both solitary reflection and lively interactions centering around the written word.

Hidden Libraries and Secret Archives:
For those seeking more clandestine experiences, hidden libraries

and secret archives promise a thrilling adventure. These are the places where historic literary treasures are carefully preserved, often accessible by invitation or appointment only. In Vatican City, the Vatican Secret Archives house centuries-old manuscripts, books, and papal correspondence that offer a fascinating glimpse into history. In New York City, the Morgan Library and Museum displays a vast collection of rare books and manuscripts, including original works by renowned authors. These hidden libraries and archives not only showcase invaluable literary works but also afford book enthusiasts the opportunity to witness the delicate art of preservation in action.

Underground Bookstores:
The allure of underground bookstores lies not only in the books they hold but also in their clandestine locations. These hidden spots are often concealed in basements or behind unassuming facades, inviting readers to uncover their secrets. In Lisbon, Portugal, the Ler Devagar bookstore occupies a converted warehouse filled with antique printing presses and winding staircases, harking back to a bygone era. In Buenos Aires, Argentina, the El Ateneo Grand Splendid bookstore enchants visitors with its neoclassical architecture, having once served as a theater. These underground bookstores not only provide respite from the outside world but also transport readers to another dimension, where literature reigns supreme.

The world is a vast treasure trove of hidden spots for book lovers to explore. Beyond the well-known bookstores and libraries, these charming nooks, literary cafes, secret archives, and underground bookstores offer unique experiences that cater to the deepest desires of bibliophiles. Whether one finds solace in a tiny bookshop nestled on a side street or immerses themselves in the grandeur of an underground literary haven, these hidden spots provide havens for book lovers to lose themselves in the magic of literature and embark on unforgettable literary adventures. So, wander off the beaten path, and let the written word guide you to these hidden gems waiting to be discovered.

Chapter 14: Religious Sites

Lesser-known churches, chapels, and religious monuments

While major religious sites like cathedrals, mosques, and temples often take center stage, there are countless lesser-known churches, chapels, and religious monuments that possess great historical, architectural, and cultural value. This one explores these hidden gems, shedding light on their significance and encouraging all to seek out their hidden beauty.

1. Understanding the Lesser-known:
In the vast tapestry of religious heritage, numerous remarkable religious sites have remained relatively unknown to the general public. Be it due to their remote locations, lack of publicity, or simply overshadowed by more famous counterparts; these lesser-known churches, chapels, and religious monuments have remained hidden in plain sight. However, beneath their unassuming façade lies a treasure trove of history, art, and spiritual significance waiting to be discovered.

2. The Allure of Lesser-known:
Exploring lesser-known churches, chapels, and religious monuments allows one to escape the crowds and experience serenity in a more personal and intimate manner. Away from the bustling tourists, these hidden gems often preserve their original

spiritual ambiance, providing visitors with a deeply immersive experience. Furthermore, the less-explored nature of these sites fosters a sense of discovery, making these visits all the more exciting and rewarding.

3. Historical and Cultural Significance:
The historical and cultural significance of lesser-known religious sites cannot be understated. They often serve as tangible links to the past, enabling us to better understand the beliefs, traditions, and lifestyles of our ancestors. These hidden treasures can shed light on the architectural styles, influences, and sociopolitical context of specific time periods, aiding historians, anthropologists, and art enthusiasts in piecing together the narrative of a bygone era.

4. Architectural Brilliance Revealed:
The diverse range of architectural styles displayed in lesser-known churches, chapels, and religious monuments is captivating and awe-inspiring. From Romanesque and Gothic to Baroque and Renaissance, these hidden structures exhibit exquisite craftsmanship, intricate ornamentation, and innovative design elements. The exploration of these hidden architectural gems not only delights the eye but also reveals the evolution of architectural techniques and influences over time.

5. Preserving Artistic Heritage:
Art holds a prominent place within the realm of religious monuments. Lesser-known churches and chapels often house exceptional artworks, including paintings, sculptures, frescoes, and stained glass windows. These artworks offer insights into the artistic styles, techniques, and subject matters of different periods, showcasing the skill of master artists. By seeking out

these hidden artistic treasures, we help preserve and celebrate humanity's artistic legacy.

6. Spiritual Retreats:
Dotted across landscapes and nestled in idyllic locales, lesser-known churches, chapels, and religious monuments offer sanctuary and refuge for spiritual seekers. Away from the commercialization and tourist activity, these hidden sites provide a serene environment for contemplation, prayer, or meditation. The connection to a higher power in these peaceful corners can be profound, providing solace, revitalization, and a chance for self-reflection.

7. Community and Local Traditions:
In addition to their spiritual and historical significance, lesser-known religious sites often remain integral to the fabric of local communities. These hidden gems serve as gathering places for religious ceremonies, festivals, and cultural events unique to the region. By participating in or witnessing these local traditions, visitors can gain a deeper understanding of the community's customs and forge meaningful connections with the people who uphold them.

In our pursuit of knowledge and exploration, it is essential not to overlook the lesser-known churches, chapels, and religious monuments that quietly exist alongside grander religious sites. Their rich history, architectural splendor, cultural relevance, and spiritual sanctity make them worthy subjects of our attention. As we peel back the layers and discover these hidden gems, we unlock a greater understanding of our collective heritage and embrace the beauty of diversity in our religious traditions.

Spiritual significance of hidden religious sites

While some places of worship are well-known and revered globally, there exist hidden religious sites that possess an aura of mystery and allure. In this discussion, we delve into the profound spiritual significance of these hidden religious sites, exploring their historical, cultural, and geographic aspects, and ultimately understanding the deeper connection between these hidden gems and the spiritual aspirations of individuals.

1. Unveiling the Mystery:
Hidden religious sites are often tucked away in remote locations or obscured by the passage of time. Their relative obscurity gives rise to an air of mystique, making them all the more enticing for those seeking a deeper spiritual experience. These secret locations are often discovered through personal revelations or passed down through generations. Their hidden nature grants them an exclusivity that adds to the spiritual weight attributed to them.

2. Historical and Cultural Context:
Hidden religious sites carry immense historical and cultural significance, encapsulating the beliefs, rituals, and traditions of specific religious communities. These sites can be regarded as tangible connections to the past, where the traces of a vibrant religious life may be preserved. For example, ancient temples etched deep into the mountainous terrains of South East Asia, or hidden Christian monastic dwellings in secluded European forests, offer glimpses into the rich cultural heritage of their respective faiths.

3. The Quest for Silence and Solitude:
Hidden religious sites often possess an inherent quality that facilitates introspection, solitude, and silence. Such elements are highly valued in many spiritual traditions, as they provide a favorable environment for deepening one's spiritual connection. Be it a hidden cave, a secret garden, or a monastery nestled amidst nature, these sites offer seekers a sanctuary of tranquility conducive to prayer, meditation, and contemplation.

4. Symbolism and Sacred Geometry:
Many hidden religious sites are designed with meticulous attention to symbolism and sacred geometry. The arrangement of sacred structures, the positioning of icons, and the integration of natural elements all contribute to the spiritual significance of these spaces. By aligning the site's architecture and layout with celestial bodies, geographical elements, or mythological symbolism, hidden religious sites evoke a heightened sense of connectedness to the divine.

5. Pilgrimage and Spiritual Journeys:
Hidden religious sites often attract seekers who embark on spiritual journeys and pilgrimages. These seekers travel to such places seeking profound spiritual experiences, hoping to deepen their understanding and connection with the divine. These holy sites become destinations that offer pilgrims a chance for transformation, healing, and spiritual renewal.

6. Spiritual Resonance and Energy:
A member of remarkable aspects of hidden religious sites is the palpable spiritual energy that emanates from them. Whether it be an ancient temple complex or a well-concealed shrine, these

sites often carry an indescribable aura that can generate a sense of awe and reverence. Many believe that the continuous devotional practices and the collective faith of countless individuals who have contributed to these sites over time imbue them with powerful spiritual energy.

Hidden religious sites offer a unique spiritual encounter for those who seek the profound. The magnetism of these hidden gems lies not only in their enigmatic allure but also in the historical, cultural, and symbolic engagements they embody. As repositories of faith and devotion, these sacred spaces play a vital role in enriching individuals' spiritual journeys by providing an opportunity for introspection, connection, and transformation. Exploring the spiritual significance of hidden religious sites encourages us to appreciate the diverse paths that lead seekers to discover the divine and enhances our understanding of the universal search for transcendence.

Chapter 15: Underground Treasures

Hidden caves, catacombs, and underground attractions

Throughout history, hidden caves have served as both refuges and repositories of ancient wisdom and artifacts. These underground chambers have been utilized by various civilizations for different purposes. Within the depths of these caves, evidence of prehistoric human settlements have been unearthed, shedding light on our ancestors' way of life. Caves were often regarded as sacred spaces, serving as places for religious ceremonies and spiritual retreats. The complexities of cave paintings and engravings found in sites such as Lascaux in France or Altamira in Spain give us a glimpse into the artistic endeavors of our early ancestors.

Catacombs, on the other hand, notably gained prominence during the Roman era, serving as underground burial sites. These vast networks of tunnels provided a solution to the overcrowding of cemeteries in densely populated areas. The catacombs of Rome, for instance, are an astounding underground complex, intricately carved out of rock, housing the remains of millions of people. Walking through these labyrinthine tunnels, one cannot help but contemplate the rich historical and cultural significance they hold.

In recent times, the allure of hidden underground attractions has expanded beyond archaeological and historical interests. These sites have become popular tourist destinations, attracting adventurers seeking unique experiences and nature enthusiasts wanting to explore untouched ecosystems. Stunning stalactites and stalagmites formed over thousands of years in caves like the Mammoth Cave in the United States or the Waitomo Glowworm Caves in New Zealand create breathtaking natural formations that are as awe-inspiring as they are fragile. The marvel of these sights lies not only in their beauty but in the knowledge that they have remained hidden from human eyes for millennia.

Aside from the natural wonders, man-made underground attractions have emerged, designed to entertain and educate visitors. One prominent example is the Catacombs of Paris, where visitors can descend beneath the bustling streets of Paris and witness this macabre network of ossuaries lined with human bones. The eerie ambiance of these underground passages serves as a stark reminder of our own mortality, inviting reflection on the passage of time.

Many hidden caves, catacombs, and underground attractions also offer unique opportunities for scientific exploration. Geologists and speleologists study these environments, seeking to unlock their secrets and gain insights into the Earth's geological processes. These explorations have led to discoveries of new species, profound understandings of climatic changes, and advancements in our knowledge of the Earth's history.

While hidden caves, catacombs, and underground attractions

offer us glimpses into the past, it is essential to emphasize the importance of responsible exploration and preservation. Many of these delicate underground environments are extremely sensitive to human interference. The impact of excessive tourism, vandalism, or neglect can cause irreversible damage. Therefore, it is crucial for visitors to follow ethical guidelines, respecting these natural and historical treasures for future generations to enjoy. From the artistic wonders of prehistoric cave paintings to the grandeur of Roman catacombs, these subterranean realms continue to captivate and inspire us. Whether for archaeological, scientific, or recreational purposes, exploring these hidden treasures conveys a sense of wonder and connects us to the beauty and secrets of the natural world. As we embark on this journey through the underground, let us remember to appreciate and protect these hidden gems, ensuring that they remain accessible for generations to come.

Unique experiences below the surface in France

One in a group of most intriguing aspects of France is its rich historical heritage, which is not limited to its famous landmarks. Beneath the streets of Paris, for example, lies a labyrinth of tunnels known as the Catacombs. Originally built as limestone quarries, these underground passages were transformed into a macabre burial ground in the late 18th century. Today, visitors can descend into the depths of the Catacombs to explore this eerie world, lined with the bones of approximately six million people. While it may not be for the faint of heart, this unique experience offers a glimpse into a different realm of French history, reminding us of the transient nature of life itself.

For those seeking a more tranquil experience, a journey along the canals of the Alsace region provides a serene escape from the bustling cities. The picturesque town of Colmar, often referred to as the "Little Venice of Alsace," is a hidden gem that deserves attention. Its narrow canals wind their way through charming medieval houses, adorned with colorful flowers. Touring the town by boat offers a unique perspective, allowing travelers to soak in the ambiance and admire the enchanting architecture from a different angle. This lesser-known destination showcases the beauty of France in a quieter, more intimate setting, inviting visitors to slow down and savor the simple pleasures of life.

Another intriguing aspect of France lies in its impressive network of underground caves. The Aven d'Orgnac in the Ardèche region is one such example, with its awe-inspiring stalactites and stalagmites. Descending into the depths of this natural wonder is like stepping into a magical realm, where centuries of geological formations have created a breathtaking spectacle. The caverns, illuminated by subtle lighting, provide a sense of wonder and mystery. Exploring these underground landscapes offers a humbling experience, reminding us of the sheer power and beauty of nature. France's subterranean wonders are a testament to the country's geological diversity and the hidden marvels that lie just below our feet.

In addition to its geological wonders, France also offers unique experiences related to its culinary traditions. The art of truffle hunting, for example, allows travelers to immerse themselves in France's gastronomic culture while exploring the picturesque countryside. In the region of Périgord, known as the "black truffle capital," visitors can join experienced truffle hunters and their dogs as they search for these elusive delicacies. This hands-on experience offers a fascinating insight into the craftsmanship and skill required to unearth these underground treasures. After a successful hunt, travelers can savor the fruits of their labor, indulging in dishes infused with the distinct earthy aroma that only the black truffle can provide. It is a truly unique and memorable way to discover the flavors that define French cuisine.

France's unique experiences below the surface add a layer of complexity and intrigue to this remarkable country. From the haunting catacombs beneath Paris to the tranquil canals of Colmar, and the subterranean wonders of caves, each discovery offers a new perspective on the country's history, beauty, and culture. Whether delving into the depths of the earth or unearthing culinary delights, these hidden gems provide an enchanting journey off the beaten path. Exploring these lesser-known aspects of France rewards the curious traveler with unforgettable memories and a deeper understanding of the country's multifaceted nature. So, venture beyond the surface and let France surprise and captivate you with its hidden treasures.

Chapter 16: Quirky Museums

Unconventional museums featuring niche collections

One example of an unconventional museum featuring a niche collection is the Museum of Bad Art (MOBA). Located in Massachusetts, MOBA is dedicated to the preservation, exhibition, and celebration of artwork that is considered to be of "questionable quality." The museum shines a light on creations that may have been rejected by traditional art institutions, encouraging viewers to challenge conventional notions of aesthetics and appreciate these pieces in a different light. By showcasing what is often deemed as "bad" art, the museum allows visitors to broaden their understanding of artistic expression and question the boundaries between good and bad art.

Another fascinating example of a museum with a niche collection is the Spoon Museum, located in Colfax, Washington. As the world's largest collection of spoons, this museum celebrates the diverse and intricate designs of this everyday household object. Visitors can browse through thousands of spoons from different eras, cultures, and materials, gaining insight into the creativity and craftsmanship involved in these seemingly mundane items. The Spoon Museum invites visitors to consider the cultural significance and historical context of spoons, challenging preconceived notions of what constitutes a valuable or thought-provoking collection.

Moving away from physical objects, there are also unconventional museums dedicated to niche collections of ideas and concepts. The Museum of Broken Relationships, founded in Croatia but with branches around the world, showcases artifacts donated by individuals following the end of their romantic relationships. Through personal items such as love letters, wedding dresses, and even a prosthetic leg, this museum tells poignant stories of heartbreak, loss, and resilience. By focusing on the emotional journey behind the objects, the Museum of Broken Relationships allows visitors to connect with universal human experiences and reflect on the complex nature of love and relationships.

In addition to thematic niche collections, there are also museums that cater to specific interests or hobbies. For example, the Dog Collar Museum in England's Leeds Castle offers a unique glimpse into the world of canine fashion and accessories. The museum displays a wide array of historical and contemporary dog collars, showcasing the diverse range of styles and materials used throughout history. This unusual collection provides dog lovers and enthusiasts with an opportunity to appreciate the beauty and craftsmanship involved in the creation of these often-overlooked accessories, as well as gain insight into changing cultural attitudes towards pets.

Unconventional museums featuring niche collections have successfully tapped into a desire for more personalized and immersive museum experiences. By focusing on specific themes or subjects, these museums offer a respite from the overwhelming nature of traditional museums that often cater to a broad audience. Visitors are provided with a curated and focused experience, allowing them to explore a particular interest while also encouraging them to question prevailing notions of what constitutes museum-worthy objects or ideas.

Furthermore, these unconventional museums open up new avenues for conversations and dialogues within the museum space. By highlighting collections that have previously been overlooked or deemed unworthy of exhibition, they challenge the hierarchical nature of the art world and museum curation. By breaking away from traditional norms, they invite visitors to engage with unconventional perspectives and challenge their own preconceptions and biases. This shift in museum experience encourages a more inclusive and diverse audience, as people from all backgrounds and interests can find a place where their curiosity is piqued and their passions are celebrated. These museums disrupt the notion of a one-size-fits-all museum experience and embrace the diversity of human knowledge, creativity, and passion. Whether it's the Museum of Bad Art, the Spoon Museum, or the Museum of Broken Relationships, these institutions provide a refreshing alternative to conventional museums, fostering engagement, appreciation, and discovery in the world of art, history, and ideas.

Hidden gems for museum enthusiasts

Institutional powerhouses like the Louvre, the British Museum, or the Smithsonian are widely known and draw millions of visitors each year. However, there is an entire world of lesser-known museums waiting to be explored by the discerning museum enthusiast. These hidden gems often offer unique and remarkable exhibits that provide a window into intriguing aspects of our shared human history. In this exploration of hidden gems for museum enthusiasts, we will delve into three fascinating and often overlooked museums: the Museo Nacional de Antropología in Mexico City, the Pergamon Museum in Berlin, and the Isabella Stewart Gardner Museum in Boston. Each of these institutions offers visitors a chance to engage with exceptional collections, providing a rich and fulfilling cultural experience.

The Museo Nacional de Antropología:

Located in the heart of Mexico City, the Museo Nacional de Antropología stands as a testament to the diverse indigenous cultures that have shaped the cultural heritage of Mexico and its people. While many tourists flock to the historic sites surrounding the Aztec and Mayan civilizations, this museum offers an immersive experience that goes beyond the ruins. Housing an extensive collection of artifacts, visitors have the opportunity to explore Mexico's vast ethnographic and archaeological history. From intricately carved Olmec stone heads to colorful Oaxacan textiles, the museum offers a glimpse into the country's rich cultural tapestry. A piece of highlights of the museum is the Hall of the Maya, where meticulously preserved ancient frescoes and ceremonial artifacts transport visitors to the world of this ancient civilization. Moreover, the museum's architecture itself is a work of art, with its iconic umbrella-like structure, designed by Pedro Ramírez Vázquez, serving as a symbol of Mexican identity. For the museum enthusiast seeking a deeper understanding of pre-Columbian civilizations, the Museo Nacional de Antropología reigns as an absolute must-visit.

The Pergamon Museum:

Situated on the Museum Island in Berlin, the Pergamon Museum stands as a crown jewel amongst the city's esteemed cultural institutions. While overshadowed by its more widely known neighbors, the Pergamon Museum offers a trinity of ancient treasures: the Pergamon Altar, the Ishtar Gate, and the Market Gate of Miletus. These monumental structures have been painstakingly reconstructed within the museum's walls, allowing visitors to step back in time and marvel at the architectural marvels of the ancient world. The Pergamon Altar, dating back to the 2nd century BC, depicts the mythical battle between the gods and the giants in captivating detail. The Ishtar Gate, originally from Babylon, transports visitors to a time of Mesopotamian splendor with its colorful glazed brick reliefs. The Market Gate of Miletus, a grand entrance to a Roman agora, offers insight into the vibrant commercial hubs of antiquity. These awe-inspiring reconstructions, accompanied by informative exhibitions and multimedia presentations, make the Pergamon Museum an essential destination for museum enthusiasts and those with a fascination for ancient civilizations.

The Isabella Stewart Gardner Museum:

Nestled in the vibrant and historic Fenway-Kenmore neighborhood of Boston, the Isabella Stewart Gardner Museum is a hidden gem that art lovers simply cannot afford to miss. Founded by the eponymous philanthropist and art collector, the museum is housed within a stunning 15th-century Venetian-style palace. Its unique setting bridges the gap between art, architecture, and horticulture, offering visitors an immersive experience like no other. The museum's collection boasts an array of masterpieces, with works by celebrated artists such as Vermeer, Botticelli, and Rembrandt. Notably, the museum is most famous for the infamous 1990 robbery, where several works were stolen, leaving empty frames still hanging on display as a poignant reminder. This captivating blend of history, art, and intrigue sets the stage for a captivating visit, allowing museum enthusiasts to transport themselves into the world of Isabella Stewart Gardner's art-filled life. With its picturesque courtyard and serene galleries, the Isabella Stewart Gardner Museum stands as a testament to the power of art and the curious spirit of museum lovers.

While the Louvres and the British Museums of the world hold undeniable allure, it is crucial for museum enthusiasts to explore the lesser-known cultural gems that exist across the globe. These hidden treasures like the Museo Nacional de Antropología in Mexico City, the Pergamon Museum in Berlin, and the Isabella Stewart Gardner Museum in Boston offer unique insights into the diverse cultural heritage of humanity. By venturing beyond the beaten path, museum enthusiasts can discover the awe-inspiring artifacts, lesser-known artists, and extraordinary stories that often go unnoticed by the masses. So, next time you find yourself embarking on a museum adventure, consider seeking out these hidden gems - you will be rewarded with an extraordinary and enriched understanding of our shared human history.

Chapter 17: Festivals and Events

Lesser-known festivals and events in France

One in a group of lesser-known festivals in France that deserves attention is the Alsatian Wine Route Festival. Nestled in the picturesque region of Alsace, this festival takes place along the famous Route des Vins (Wine Route) which stretches across about 170 kilometers, encompassing charming villages and breathtaking vineyards. The festival occurs annually in early summer, celebrating the region's exceptional winemaking heritage. Visitors can immerse themselves in the convivial atmosphere of the festival, savoring the finest Alsatian wines, and delighting in the traditional gastronomy Alsace has to offer. With live music performances, vineyard tours, and wine tastings, this festival provides an excellent opportunity to experience the genuine charm of this lesser-explored part of France.

Another noteworthy event is the Festival of Lights in Lyon. Held every December, this dazzling celebration transforms the city into a sparkling wonderland. Originating from a religious tradition dating back to the 1800s, the festival later evolved into a stunning display of lights, illuminating Lyon's streets, squares, and historical landmarks. Every year, millions of visitors flock to Lyon to witness this magical spectacle. The city becomes a living art gallery, with mesmerizing light installations and projections that adorn buildings and public spaces. The festival has gained international recognition, but remains slightly under the radar compared to other renowned light festivals. The Festival of Lights is a perfect example of a lesser-known event that unveils the brilliance and creativity of France's cultural scene.

For enthusiasts of traditional folklore, the Carnival of Dunkirk in the northern region of Hauts-de-France is an absolute must-see. This boisterous and lively carnival is deeply rooted in the local fishing community's history and customs. From January to March, the streets of Dunkirk come alive with processions, colorful parades, and plenty of music and dance. The carnival features distinctive characters such as the "Carnival Giant" and the "Klouk," who symbolize the spirit of the festival. These figures are accompanied by revelers donning eccentric costumes and masks, creating a festive atmosphere filled with laughter and joy. The Carnival of Dunkirk is a lesser-known gem that provides an authentic insight into the proud cultural traditions of this coastal region.

Moving southwards, we come across the Corsican polyphonic singing festival, A Filetta. Held in the charming town of Pigna, perched high in the mountains of Corsica, this festival celebrates the unique form of polyphonic singing that is deeply ingrained in Corsican culture. Every summer, musicians and singers from all over the island gather to showcase their talents and share their passion for this hauntingly beautiful music. The festival not only offers captivating performances, but it also provides opportunities for visitors to engage in workshops and learn about the history and significance of Corsican polyphonic traditions. A Filetta festival represents the essence of lesser-known events, showcasing the heart and soul of regional cultural heritage. The Alsatian Wine Route Festival, the Festival of Lights in Lyon, the Carnival of Dunkirk, and the Corsican polyphonic singing festival, A Filetta, are just a small selection of the many hidden gems that showcase the cultural diversity and richness of France. These events go beyond the iconic celebrations, allowing travelers to delve into the authentic traditions and local customs of different regions of the country. So, next time you plan a trip to France, consider exploring these lesser-known festivals, and embark on a remarkable journey through the heart and soul of this enchanting nation.

Cultural celebrations off the beaten path

One such celebration is the Yi Peng Lantern Festival in Thailand. While many visitors are familiar with Thailand's vibrant Songkran water festival, the Yi Peng Lantern Festival remains somewhat under the radar. Held annually in the northern city of Chiang Mai, this festival involves the release of thousands of lanterns into the night sky. The sight of these glowing lanterns ascending towards the heavens creates a mesmerizing spectacle, symbolizing the release of negative energy and the embracing of new beginnings. Participants write their wishes and aspirations on the lanterns before releasing them, making it a deeply personal and meaningful experience. Beyond the visual spectacle, the Yi Peng Lantern Festival also plays a crucial role in promoting unity among communities, as families and friends come together to celebrate and share in the experience.

Moving to the African continent, one may encounter the Gerewol Festival in Chad, which is an extraordinary celebration of beauty and courtship among the Wodaabe people. This festival provides a rare opportunity to witness a traditional beauty contest where men are the participants. Men spend days meticulously preparing themselves for this grand event, adorning themselves with elaborate costumes, applying face paint, and curling their hair using cow horns soaked in water. They compete through the performance of traditional dances, showcasing their agility, charm, and attractiveness. The women, who serve as the judges, evaluate their potential future partners based on these criteria. Aside from its captivating visual aspect, the Gerewol Festival showcases the unique cultural practices of the Wodaabe people, offering outsiders a glimpse into their values, customs, and social dynamics.

A less-known celebration that holds profound cultural significance is the Obon Festival in Japan. Originating from Buddhist traditions, this mid-summer festival is a time when families honor their ancestors and pay respects to the departed souls. During Obon, it is believed that the spirits of ancestors return to visit their living relatives. To welcome and guide them, families light lanterns and float them on rivers or release them into the sea, creating a breathtaking spectacle of flickering lights. Additionally, traditional dances called "bon odori" are performed at community gatherings, providing an opportunity for people to come together, express gratitude, and connect with their cultural heritage. The Obon Festival not only strengthens familial bonds but also serves as a reminder of the importance of acknowledging and honoring one's roots.

Venturing into the highlands of Papua New Guinea, one encounters the Mount Hagen Cultural Show, a colorful display of tribal traditions, art, and music. Situated in the Western Highlands Province, this annual festival brings together various tribes that reside in the region, each showcasing their vibrant cultural heritage. Participants dress in exquisite traditional attire, adorned with intricate face paintings, headdresses, and ornaments. The festival is a platform for these tribes to demonstrate their unique dances, rituals, and ceremonies, preserving and promoting their traditions for future generations. Visitors have the privilege of witnessing the diverse cultural tapestry that makes up Papua New Guinea, immersing themselves in a world that is unlike anything found in mainstream society.

These mentioned cultural celebrations are merely a glimpse into the vast array of offbeat festivities that exist worldwide. Each celebration represents an opportunity to learn, appreciate, and participate in cultural practices that are not readily accessible to outsiders. Taking part in these events fosters cross-cultural understanding and promotes mutual respect by challenging preconceived notions and embracing the beauty of diversity. By venturing off the beaten path, individuals not only enrich their own lives but also contribute to the preservation and continuation of cultural traditions that might otherwise fade away in an increasingly globalized world.

Chapter 18: Conclusion

Reflection on the importance of uncovering hidden gems in France

France. The mere mention of this majestic country invokes images of the Eiffel Tower, the Louvre, and the charming cafes that line the streets of Paris. But beyond these well-known landmarks lies a treasure trove of hidden gems waiting to be discovered. Uncovering these lesser-known wonders is not only a thrilling adventure, but it also allows us to gain a deeper understanding and appreciation of French culture, history, and natural beauty. In this reflection, we will explore the importance of uncovering these hidden gems in France, and the enriching experiences they offer.

One compelling reason to seek out hidden gems in France is the opportunity to escape the crowded tourist destinations and explore the authentic essence of the country. While landmarks like the Eiffel Tower undoubtedly hold their own allure, they can often be overrun with tourists, making it difficult to fully immerse oneself in the true French experience. It is in the hidden gems that we find respite from the tourist crowds and discover the heart of France. Whether it be a quaint village tucked away in the countryside, an ancient castle lost in time, or a serene beach along the coastline, these hidden gems offer a genuine glimpse into the lives of the French people and allow us to forge meaningful connections with locals.

Uncovering hidden gems in France not only allows for a more authentic experience but also enriches our understanding of the country's history and cultural heritage. France, with its rich history dating back centuries, boasts numerous lesser-known sites that carry stories of forgotten eras and extraordinary pasts. Exploring medieval villages with their cobblestone streets, ancient churches, and impressive ruins takes us on a journey through time. These hidden gems provide a unique perspective on the historical events and cultural influences that have shaped France throughout the ages. By delving into the lesser-known aspects of French history, we gain a more comprehensive understanding of the country and the people who call it home.

It is also in the hidden gems of France that we encounter the country's natural wonders, showcasing its diverse landscapes and breathtaking beauty. From the rugged cliffs of the Normandy coast to the idyllic vineyards of the Burgundy region, France's natural landscapes have captivated artists, writers, and explorers for centuries. By venturing off the beaten path, we have the opportunity to witness these natural wonders in their unadulterated state. Whether we are hiking through the picturesque countryside, kayaking along tranquil rivers, or strolling through hidden gardens, these experiences allow us to reconnect with nature and appreciate the immense beauty that France has to offer.

In addition to the enriching experiences and deeper understanding of the country, uncovering hidden gems in France also contributes to sustainable tourism. While popular tourist destinations are often the lifeblood of the travel industry, they can also put a strain on local resources, infrastructure, and culture. The pursuit of hidden gems encourages a more balanced distribution of tourism, reducing the burden on heavily trafficked areas and fostering economic development in other, less-visited regions. By supporting local businesses, staying in family-run accommodations, and participating in community-based initiatives, we play an active role in sustainable tourism practices. Uncovering hidden gems in France not only benefits us as travelers but also ensures the preservation of these gems for future generations to enjoy. These hidden gems offer an authentic French experience, providing us with a deeper understanding and appreciation of this remarkable country. As we embark on this exploration, let us embrace the thrill of discovery and cherish the hidden treasures that lie waiting to be uncovered in every corner of France.

Encouragement to continue exploring lesser-known destinations.

A member of primary reasons to embark on a journey to lesser-known destinations is the opportunity to experience the allure of untouched beauty. Many of these hidden gems boast landscapes and natural wonders that remain unspoiled by mass tourism. Imagine stumbling upon a secluded beach with turquoise waters and powdery white sand, or witnessing the breathtaking grandeur of a pristine mountain range devoid of crowds. These destinations offer an escape from the hustle and bustle of popular touristic hotspots, allowing travelers to reconnect with nature and find solace in the peacefulness that surrounds them. By venturing into these lesser-known destinations, we can be awestruck by the sheer beauty and tranquility that nature has to offer.

In addition to untouched beauty, exploring lesser-known destinations provides a unique opportunity to immerse oneself in an authentic cultural encounter. Popular tourist destinations often undergo commercialization in order to cater to the overwhelming influx of visitors. This commercialization can result in a loss of cultural identity and the commodification of local traditions. On the other hand, lesser-known destinations tend to retain their authenticity, providing travelers with an invaluable chance to engage with local communities, traditions, and ways of life. By conversing with locals, trying traditional cuisine, and partaking in cultural activities, travelers can gain a deeper understanding and appreciation of the destination they are exploring. These authentic experiences create lifelong memories and contribute to a broader understanding and acceptance of diverse cultures.

Moreover, venturing into lesser-known destinations allows travelers to uncover hidden histories and untold stories. Many popular tourist destinations have well-documented histories that are widely disseminated and easily accessible. Yet lesser-known destinations harbor hidden layers of history and tradition, waiting to be uncovered by curious souls. These destinations often hold historical landmarks, archaeological sites, or cultural relics that have been overlooked by mainstream tourism. By delving into the depths of these destinations' histories, travelers have the privilege of unearthing forgotten narratives and gaining a deeper understanding of the world's diverse heritage. This exploration not only enriches personal knowledge but also contributes to the preservation and appreciation of these lesser-known destinations' cultural and historical significance.

Additionally, venturing into lesser-known destinations can have a profound impact on sustainable and responsible tourism practices. Popular tourist destinations are often strained by the pressures of mass tourism, leading to environmental degradation, overcrowding, and social challenges. By diverting our attention and resources to lesser-known destinations, we can distribute the benefits of tourism more equitably and alleviate the strain on heavily visited areas. This shift promotes sustainable development, encourages local communities to take pride in their heritage, and drives economic growth in marginalized regions. Furthermore, exploring lesser-known destinations with a responsible mindset allows travelers to support local businesses, engage in eco-friendly practices, and ensure that the destination remains preserved for future generations to experience. By encouraging travelers to explore these hidden gems, we promote sustainable and responsible tourism practices, foster cultural understanding, and contribute to the preservation of our planet's diverse heritage. Through venturing off the beaten path, we can embark on a transformative journey filled with awe-inspiring landscapes, immersive cultural encounters, and untold narratives. So, let us be inspired to continue exploring these lesser-known destinations, as the rewards they offer far transcend the boundaries of popular tourist hotspots.

Printed in Dunstable, United Kingdom